Simple

Simple

Conquering the Crisis
of Complexity

Alan Siegel and Irene Etzkorn

TWELVE

NEW YORK   BOSTON

Twelve
Hachette Book Group
237 Park Avenue
New York, NY 10017

www.HachetteBookGroup.com

Printed in the United States of America

RRD-C

First Edition: April 2013
10 9 8 7 6 5 4 3 2 1

Twelve is an imprint of Grand Central Publishing.
The Twelve name and logo are trademarks of Hachette Book Group, Inc.

The Hachette Speakers Bureau provides a wide range of authors for
speaking events. To find out more, go to
www.hachettespeakersbureau.com or call (866) 376-6591.

The publisher is not responsible for websites (or their content)
that are not owned by the publisher.

Library of Congress Cataloging-in-Publication Data
Siegel, Alan M. (Alan Michael), 1938–
Simple / Alan Siegel and Irene Etzkorn.—First Edition.
    pages cm
Includes bibliographical references.
    ISBN 978-1-4555-0966-9 (hbk.)—ISBN 978-1-4555-0968-3 (ebk.)—
ISBN 978-1-61113-721-7 (audio download)   1. Business writing.   2. Legal
composition.   I. Etzkorn, Irene.   II. Title.
    HF5718.3.S54 2013
    808.06'665—dc23
                                                                    2012041983

We dedicate this book to our clients who had the courage to fight for simplicity when the path of least resistance was to perpetuate complexity. A rare breed of visionaries, they inspire us to keep questioning, challenging, editing, and streamlining. Specifically, we admire:

Charles Luchs
(formerly of Chubb Insurance)

Anthony DeMeo
(formerly of Shearson Lehman)

Jodi Patterson and Denise Fayne
at Internal Revenue Service

Joseph Clark
(formerly of Lincoln Life Insurance)

Carl Felsenfeld and Duncan McDonald
(formerly of Citibank)

CONTENTS

Contents

INTRODUCTION

There are two simplicity warriors writing this book. Alan Siegel became one by accident in 1975. Irene Etzkorn became one deliberately in 1981. Here is a bit of context for why we are writing this book together and at this moment.

When I, Alan, started a corporate design firm, I was determined to go beyond graphics (logos and color palettes) by fusing strategy, content, and design to reflect the distinctive corporate voice of each client. Having started the firm with a loan from the Venture Capital Group of First National City Bank (the predecessor of Citibank), I had built a relationship with the marketing department of their retail bank. They asked me to redesign their customer forms—applications, signature cards, loan notes—to reinforce their desired image as a global banking leader.

The shock of seeing their installment loan note made it clear to me that design was not the issue or the solution. Riddled with dense legalese, the contract screamed, "Don't read this!" But it also communicated a great business opportunity. The bank viewed it as a "necessary evil" and just a bit of "paperwork," but I saw something more. I told them not to waste time and money on a cosmetic redesign but to let me question the content with their lawyers, rewrite it in plain English, and then design a document that could build the reputation of the bank and convey a message of wanting to expand relationships with customers, not turn them off.

Having attended law school just long enough to take a first-year course in contracts, I believed that a clearer, more useful contract was achievable. I secured a modest budget from the marketing folks despite their lack of enthusiasm (they were betting on their lawyers killing my work somewhere in the drafting stage). I called in Dr. Rudolf Flesch, an Austrian immigrant with a PhD from Columbia who was an expert on readability and the author of *The Art of Readable Writing*. He was thrilled at the prospect of applying his concepts to a heavy-duty legal contract for a world-class bank, and together we dissected the note and created a streamlined outline. He then rewrote it using shorter sentences, personal pronouns, a logical structure, and more familiar terminology. The well-organized, clearly written draft was then designed to be accessible and visually inviting. Judge it for yourself.

Here is the original default clause:

In the event of default in the payment of this or any other Obligation or the performance or observance of any term or covenant contained herein or in any note or other contract or agreement evidencing or relating to any Obligation or any Collateral on the Borrower's part to be performed or observed; or the undersigned Borrower shall die; or any of the undersigned become insolvent or make an assignment for the benefit of creditors; or a petition shall be filed by or against any of the undersigned under any provision of the Bankruptcy Act; or any money, securities or property of the undersigned now or hereafter on deposit with or in possession or under the control of the bank shall be attached or become subject to distraint proceedings or any order or process of any court; or the Bank shall deem itself to be insecure then and in any such event the bank shall have the right (at its option), without demand or notice of any kind, to declare all or any part of the Obligations to be immediately due and payable, whereupon such obligations shall become and be immediately due and payable, and the Bank shall have the right to exercise all the rights and remedies available to a secured party upon default under the Uniform Commercial Code (the "Code") in effect in New York at the time, and such other rights and remedies as may otherwise be provided by law.

... and here is how we rewrote it:

> I'll be in default:
> 1. If I don't pay an installment on time; or
> 2. If any other creditor tries by legal process to take any money of mine in your possession.

That was it. We learned the valuable lesson that the content must be questioned first, before rewriting. In this case, we revealed that the most important issue that triggered default was a failure to pay on time, and the rewrite emphasized that effectively.

Fast-forwarding to the happy ending, what the bank's marketing department received was a shorter, readable, inviting document that has stood the test of time, while I launched a new line of business: simplification.

During the months of endless meetings and revisions, I had gained a new perspective. Everywhere I looked, I found complexity that had a dramatic, negative impact on people's lives. I realized that business and government would achieve enormous benefits from simplicity, while consumers and citizens would become better informed. Coupled with the media attention that our work on the simplified loan note drew, the plain English movement emerged. Rapidly, several states passed plain English laws, and the Practicing Law Institute scheduled a series of educational programs. On March 23, 1978, President Jimmy Carter signed Executive Order 12044, calling for federal regulations to be understandable to their intended audiences.

At the same time, we were part of a consortium that received a grant from the National Institute of Education. One part of the grant was given to Carnegie-Mellon University to develop academic degrees in related fields. Irene Etzkorn, who would turn out to share my passion for simplicity but not my short temper, was a graduate of the first class of the resulting Master of Arts in Professional Writing program. Where I had worked by trial and error and on instinct, Irene brought academic training. With courses in rhetorical theory, linguistics, cognitive psychology, professional and technical writing, and graphic design, Irene brought the interdisciplinary perspective that was vital to expanding the concept of simplification beyond business documents. Ultimately touching all media (print, online, voice) and every industry (medicine, finance, manufacturing, technology), Irene has created many of the methodologies and techniques that have become the definition of simplification.

The guiding force behind the expansion of simplicity from a corporate frill to a business necessity, Irene brought structure and rigor to a new area of communication. So from here on in this book, our shared voice will be expressed as "we," in keeping with our harmonized appreciation for simplicity and our joint vision for its potential to change our society for the better.

Much in the same way that the seminal loan note project and the resulting media attention created a perfect storm in the 1970s, we believe that 2013 is another pivotal moment. The ubiquity of social media, coupled with consumer distrust of big business and governmental pressure for greater transparency, makes this a watershed time for our society. Consumers are beginning to fight back almost instantaneously through Twitter, Facebook, and blogs when they sense that a company is hoodwinking them through a fog of fine print.

This book reflects our shared vision about the critical importance of simplicity today—in the business world, in government, in our daily lives. For both Irene and me, this is a passion and a cause to which we've committed ourselves fully. We hope that by the time you finish reading this book, you'll feel as strongly about the value of simplicity as we do and will refuse to accept the complexity that inhibits informed decision making, puts your health at risk, endangers your family's safety, and places you in a financial hole.

Simple

PART I

The Antidote to Complexity

CHAPTER 1

....

The Crisis of Complexity

How'd We Get into This Mess?

COMPLEXITY IS WREAKING HAVOC ON BUSINESS,
GOVERNMENT, AND FINANCE.

In 1980, the typical credit card contract was about a page and a half long. *Today it is thirty-one pages.* The consequence is that people no longer read these agreements, then find their accounts canceled or subject to high interest rates.

■ **Landline phone customers paid more than $2 billion a year for unauthorized charges,** according to 2011 FCC estimates, largely because the bills are so confusing that most customers "never realized they were being charged."[1] Of course they didn't realize it. What is the difference between "Basic," "Regional," "Non-Basic," and "All Other" charges? Not to mention that there are eleven separate taxes, fees, and "other charges" that amount to almost 50 percent of a typical wireless phone bill.

- Homeowners spend an average of $868 per year for homeowner's insurance without understanding what they've bought. A 2007 National Association of Insurance Commissioners (NAIC) survey revealed that **one-third to one-half of insurance policyholders were misinformed** about what perils are covered and how much they might receive if they made a claim. The study included 673 respondents interviewed by phone with a margin of error of 3.8 percent at a 95 percent level of confidence.

- **Marquis Dunson died in 2002 after his parents gave the one-year-old Infants' Tylenol** for three days to treat his cold symptoms.[2] In the subsequent lawsuit, which resulted in a $5 million award, the plaintiffs argued that the warning labels and directions on the Infants' Tylenol label did not make clear that an overdose of acetaminophen, Tylenol's active ingredient, could lead to liver failure. The FDA estimates that an average of 458 deaths each year are due to acetaminophen overdoses.

- *Southern Medical Journal* published a study that estimated **a dermatologist signs his or her name 29,376 times a year.**[3] Can someone do anything thirty thousand times a year with focus and certainty?

- The United States was founded and governed for over two centuries on the basis of a document that is

six pages long. That is 0.1 percent of the length of the current income tax code, which currently runs a whopping fourteen thousand pages.

What do these stories have in common? They're among many examples of how complexity is costing us money, undermining government and business, and putting our health and even our lives at risk. Our current crisis of complexity is just now beginning to be the subject of a percolating public debate. The first stirrings and rumblings are being voiced in the form of op-eds, tweets, and blogs challenging the notion that disclosing information is the same as informing people. Merely telling consumers that they are being taken advantage of does not solve the underlying injustice. It is at best a halfway measure. But for the most part, how are we as citizens, patients, businesspeople, consumers, investors, borrowers, and students responding? With complacency.

We have allowed complexity to get the better of us—permitted companies, organizations, governments, and institutions to overwhelm our good judgment and violate our basic rights. We have passively paid when faced with indecipherable fees and ignored dozens of myste-

> *"Anything simple always interests me."*
> —DAVID HOCKNEY

rious features on gadgets we can't figure out how to use. We find ourselves lost in multilayered phone trees and jumping through hoops to make insurance claims.

All of which raises the question: Why do we tolerate complexity in our lives? Most of us figure we don't have a choice. We may even occasionally blame ourselves for being overwhelmed and confused. ("This is over my head, I must be an idiot.") So we pay the occasional overdraft fee of $34 that strikes us as unfair and certainly annoying, but not devastating. We don't see the ice age of complexity approaching in the distance, because we only experience small blizzards of paperwork. So we trudge along, hoping that we're not *too* misinformed and that we're not getting cheated *too* badly.

It doesn't have to be that way.

There is a powerful antidote and a practical answer within our grasp. It can be summed up in a word: **simplicity**.

What is simplicity?

There's nothing simple about simplicity. It is a concept with many nuances and lines. A second pass suggests that clarity makes for simplicity—something with clear intent that quickly conveys its purpose or use. With even greater magnification, you find that it's about essence—cutting to what matters, delivering substantive content that seems to speak to an audience of one. Lastly, it's not about what is there but what you take—a feeling of confidence, of trust, of satisfaction. So for us, simplicity has no synonym—it's not just convenience, clarity, usability, timeliness, or beauty. It's the sum of all of those, and that's why it is so rare. When you reach a point where you have achieved **transparency** (laying bare the underlying truth whatever it reveals), **clarity** (expressing meaning clearly and simply), and **usability** (making something fit for its purpose), you have likely achieved simplicity.

Making things simple requires dedication to clarity, honesty, discipline, and intelligence. Some of the great minds in history have understood this.

In the twenty-first century, Steve Jobs emerged as one of the great champions of simplicity. While other companies complicated their gadgets with proliferating bells

> *"Simplicity is the ultimate sophistication."*
> —LEONARDO DA VINCI

and whistles, Apple succeeded by anticipating users' needs through streamlining and paring down—one button replacing three, and easy-to-understand icons in place of techie jargon. John Sculley, the former president of Apple, observed that Jobs was a minimalist who was "constantly reducing things to the simplest level." But Sculley made a careful distinction: "Not simplistic—simplified."[4] The point is that there is a world of difference between simple and simplistic. The distinction lies in understanding what is essential and meaningful as opposed to what is not, then ruthlessly eliminating the latter, while putting emphasis and focus on the former.

Through the years, we have come to believe in simplicity as

a philosophy, a guiding principle, and a way of life. And based on our experience, we believe that:

Simplicity works—in business, in government, in life.

Everyone needs it more now than ever. People can and should demand it.

- Over **425,000 apps** in the Apple iPhone App Store

- **241 selections** on the Cheesecake Factory menu, not including lunch or brunch specials

- **223 mascaras, 454 lotions**, and **367 fragrances** at Sephora

- **14,568 diagnostic codes** maintained by the Centers for Medicare and Medicaid Services

- **111 pages** in the average credit card agreement

A crisis of complexity has escalated to a critical point where a decision must be made. We either relinquish the power to understand and control what affects us, or we fight for a better, simpler way to conduct our daily affairs and our commercial transactions. This book is meant to explain the wide-ranging applications of simplicity—how it works and why it benefits us. But we also hope it will serve as a call to action: the spark for a movement toward reduction of societal, governmental, and corporate complexity.

If you're fed up with the fine print that hinders you every

day or you're a businessperson who wants to get closer to customers instead of alienating them with complicated products, policies, and communications, then you are a prime candidate for this movement.

On the other hand, if you're a bureaucrat who revels in red tape or a lawyer who loves dense legal jargon, consider yourself forewarned. This book aims to demystify what you do, expose the reasons why you do it, and make it a lot harder to keep doing it.

After the Citibank success that launched simplification as a business for us, people started coming to our company with projects from all kinds of businesses, even Uncle Sam himself. We were hired to simplify forms for the U.S. Census Bureau, as well as the Internal Revenue Service (with whom we developed the simplified 1040EZ single-page tax form). We began to develop a reputation as simplification specialists (so much so that Alan Siegel was dubbed "Mr. Plain English" by *People* magazine[5]).

> *"I would not give a fig for the simplicity this side of complexity, but I would give my life for the simplicity on the other side of complexity."*
> —OLIVER WENDELL HOLMES

Alan worked with Carnegie-Mellon University to establish a Communications Design Center that combined communications theory, cognitive research, and corporate assignments to make students aware that there was a new occupation emerging.

We developed and refined a Simplification Blueprint methodology and established a Simplicity Lab, where concepts and communications are tested to see if they're clear and understandable. The Blueprint is a strategic view of how and when to communicate, looking at the dimensions of speed, media, tone, format, and level of customization. The Simplicity Lab is an online tool that allows us to determine actual comprehension while evaluating people's perception of simplicity. For the past thirty years, we've been out there on the front lines, witnessing firsthand how companies, government agencies, and everyday people are coping with the crisis of complexity.

We've learned several invaluable lessons.

We refuted the erroneous belief that simplicity was "dumbing down" by continually stressing that it is an effective shorthand for clarity, accessibility, and usability, which benefits everyone, not just those with limited literacy or education.

We became skeptical of legislating simplicity. All too often, government bureaucrats want to establish readability formulas as the standard of comprehension or use all uppercase, bold type as a means of emphasis. In our risk-averse society, this had shifted the focus from true communication and consumer understanding to one of compliance with the law while failing to achieve its spirit.

We realized that going back to a blank slate is critical. The key to breakthrough simplicity is to question the content and make sure it reflects reality. Throw out unenforceable provisions, question outdated business practices, challenge inertia.

We discovered that the principles of simplicity apply to every interaction, whether printed, electronic, verbal, or visual. It doesn't matter whether it is a contract, an instruction, a touchscreen, or a phone tree. Whether it is a prompt

> *"Everything should be made as simple as possible but not simpler."*
> —ALBERT EINSTEIN

on a bank ATM, the wording of a prescription label, or the graphics on a global positioning device, it is a form of communication. Products of all types—appliances, vehicles, medicines, foods—and services whether provided by a hotel, a hospital, or an online retailer can benefit from simplicity.

We found that simplification provides significant business benefits in the form of cost savings, better client retention, enhanced employee efficiency, and competitive advantage for first movers.

We don't view complexity as a necessary evil. We see it as a thief that must be apprehended. It robs us of time, patience, understanding, money, and optimism. We're always looking for clues as to why something became so convoluted, what the motive was—and how the culprit can be stopped before doing more harm.

As for simplicity, we think of it as the essence of the golden rule. Everyone wants to understand what is being offered or expected of them, and simplicity helps make that clear. It shortens the distance between people. It's about building humanity

> *"The busier life gets, the more value there is in simplicity as a point of competitive differentiation."*
>
> —ARKADI KUHLMANN, CEO OF ING DIRECT USA

into everything you do, whether you're communicating with people, designing products, or delivering services. It indicates that we've taken the time to move the complexity of something out of the way so that the recipient of an object, a deed, a gesture, or a letter understands what we mean. It can also be a thing of structural beauty. Conveying a lot of information in a tight bundle is as elegant as a biological taxonomy (kingdom, phylum, class, order, family, genus, species). If every living creature can be identified with just seven classifications, why shouldn't we be able to similarly distill anything?

Following the golden rule—all well and good. But simplicity is also a bottom-line issue in business. As you'll see through the numerous case studies, companies that simplify their products, services, and communications are able to improve their relationship with customers. They usually are more productive—because when you make things simple and clear for customers, you spend less time having to answer their questions on customer service lines. These businesses are also more efficient, taking a less-is-more approach. Streamlining operations cuts costs and brings more focus to the company and its mission. And it also invariably provides a better overall experience for the consumer.

As critical as it is in business, simplicity is not just a business issue—it's an everyday life issue, among people struggling to deal with government bureaucracy, confusion in the medical realm, indecipherable bills and applications, shady contracts, feature-laden products. The human toll caused by these problems begins at birth and runs the gamut from college students drowning in loan agreements to senior citizens unable to access their Medicare benefits. There is nothing that cannot be made simpler.

So why, then, is complexity winning?

There isn't a short answer. There are various social forces, popular misconceptions, attitudes, and motivations that either let complexity fester or actively oppress simplicity. These problem areas cross the lines between business, government, and private life—because the same forces that cause complexity in one area also cause it in another.

On the principle that one must know what causes a problem before you can begin to solve it, here are some of the key factors fueling the complexity crisis.

Simplicity is hard to achieve

It takes work to organize, streamline, clarify, and generally make sense of the world around us. People are naturally more inclined to take the easy way out—one that doesn't involve such onerous tasks as going through multiple design cycles to make a product as simple as possible. This human impulse to find the path of least resistance is at work on the part of both companies and customers. Similarly, many engineers get enamored of their own creativity and keep adding features just because they can, not because they have verified consumer need for the feature.

To be sure, it is easier to ignore or tolerate complexity than to battle it—but only at first. Gradually, this "easier" path we've chosen grows so cluttered with complication that it becomes difficult to move ahead, and eventually, the path is gone— completely overgrown. That's where we are now.

Learned helplessness

As human beings, we are programmed to learn from our experiences. When faced with certain limitations over and over again, our brains begin to perceive these limitations as permanent restrictions, even if they're removed. When someone has several experiences of being confused, that person starts assuming they'll never be able to understand any legal document, so why bother trying? This results in what psychologists refer to as "learned helplessness." Trap a bee in a jar long enough and it will stop trying to fly out, even after the cap is removed.

To some extent, we may even be inclined to put our trust in complexity, developing a sort of "master" complex. The *New York Times* journalist David Segal observed that when we encounter "ideas and objects that are hard to understand," we are likely to assume that these complicated offers are the product of "sharp impressive minds."[6] Don't bet on it. A sharp mind could have articulated the offer in an accessible manner. Complexity is a failing, unless it was intentional—in which case you'd really better watch your step.

Complexity is used as a moneymaking tactic

Some companies willfully create complexity. The disturbing truth is that banks, credit card companies, insurers, and other types of businesses find ways to make money from the fine print nobody can read or understand. They use the confusion to slip in terms and conditions that they'd rather you didn't notice.

The use of complexity as a cloak not only has adverse effects on individuals; it has huge ramifications for society. Concealed terms in loans and mortgages can lead to defaults, which wreak havoc on our economy. Complexity has been a useful tool of scam artists as well as "innovators" who gave us collateralized debt obligations and other financial hazards. To quote the eminent British historian and author Paul Johnson, the cloaking effects of complexity enable companies and individuals to "conceal bad judgment, incompetence, and unconscionable risk-taking."[7]

Complexity is also used as a shield

To avoid lawsuits or other potential problems, lawyers have inundated us with mind-numbing disclaimers, disclosures, terms, instructions, amendments, and amendments to amendments. The basic thinking here is that to be safe, one must address every possibility, no matter how remote. Insurance industry consumer advocate and professor of law Daniel Schwarcz cites the "particular culture of conservativism, lack of change, and protection of information" that goes into contract writing. When battling against insurance companies for transparency and reform, he says, "You hear a lot of claims like, 'All that's going to do is promote litigation—more class action and nonmeritorious suits'... without too much thought about in which cases that might actually be [true]."[8]

Complexity gets worse over time; it builds upon itself

"Complexity creeps up on you," observes Joseph Tainter, an anthropologist at the University of Utah, whose book *The Collapse of Complex Societies* illustrates that complexity may have been the ultimate downfall of the historic enlightened cultures.[9] A major reason for the constant buildup is that no one seems to want to take the trouble to gut the system and start fresh. Companies and governments find it easier to just keep amending and adding on, sometimes to laws or policies that are irrelevant or of unknown derivation.

Consider the U.S. tax code, for example. It has nearly tripled in volume during the last decade, from 1.4 million words to 3.8 million, according to the national taxpayer advocate and ombudsman for the IRS Nina E. Olson, who estimates that Americans spend 6.1 billion hours preparing returns (the equivalent of three million employees, working full-time).[10] And on top of that, complexity causes accidental underpayments and encourages cheating—more than a trillion dollars in write-offs, loopholes, and deductions. Thanks to all the confusion, according to IRS Publication 4822, *Taxpayer Filing Attribute Report*, almost 60 percent of taxpayers hire someone to prepare their tax return, and 32 percent use tax preparation software. Even IRS commissioner Douglas Shulman admitted on C-SPAN's *Newsmakers* that he can't do his personal return anymore because "it's just too complicated."[11]

People mistakenly believe that more information equals greater clarity

From jury instructions to instruction manuals, we're witnessing an epidemic of overexplaining. This seems to be based on the fallacy that if you provide people with more information, it will yield greater understanding. In fact, the opposite is true: Too much information overwhelms people. It creates fuzziness, not clarity. When inundated with information, people are apt to lose sight of what's important and stop paying attention.

One of the more stark illustrations of this phenomenon involves Supreme Court decisions. It turns out that the longer these written decisions become, the less clear they are. In 1954, the historic *Brown v. Board of Education* decision was less than four thousand words; in 2007, the Roberts Supreme Court revisited just one aspect of that case—and ended up publishing a forty-seven-thousand-word explanation of its decision. And this was not an aberration. A recent *New York Times* report noted that the median length of majority opinions reached an all-time high in the last term. Yet—and here's the kicker—with all of that extra verbiage, judicial experts say the decisions ended up being "fuzzy" and "unwieldy," and often failed to provide clear guidelines to the lower courts.[12]

The lawyers rule

We learned this early, in that first simplification job we did for First National City Bank. Yes, we ended up simplifying their documents, and yes, the customers loved it. But the involvement of two key lawyers who supported the idea of simplicity was critical to the overall success of the project.

Here, we learned a valuable lesson about a chief cause of complexity—the legal system. Lawyers often insist that any attempt to simplify language runs the risk of failing to comply with regulations. But in fact many plain-language legal documents have been put into use.

The problem (which affects not only banks, but all large businesses and government) involves a compulsion among lawyers to use complex language and terminology to articulate every possible scenario. Lawyers invoke the specter of class action lawsuits, and everything else becomes secondary. They insist that using "legalese" is the only safe way to communicate, and in so doing, they break down communication.

The excerpt from a health insurance contract shown in Figure 1.1 is difficult for anyone to understand, whether they are a lawyer or a layperson. Using the word "not" three times and "included" twice in one sentence creates a brain twister. It seems hard to defend that this is communication.

If you ask businesses why they defer to Legal on these critical matters of communication, they tell you that there is a great deal of money at stake. We agree—companies are losing a good deal of that money by *not* simplifying communications with consumers.

More than 80 percent of respondents in a recent survey said banks should simplify paperwork for credit cards and loans.[13] For businesses, the benefits of simplicity lie in retaining customers who buy more products from them because they trust that the company is being straightforward about the value. Similarly, employees are more comfortable selling products and services that they understand.

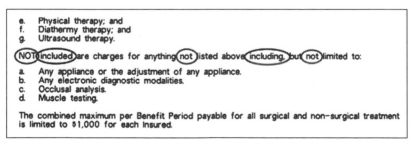

Figure 1.1   The stranglehold of legalese. Using the word "not" three times and "included" twice in one sentence creates a brain twister.

Jargon prevails

To connect with people, you have to speak their language. The use of jargon represents a decision on the part of companies and government to speak in a language that they understand and you don't.

This isn't necessarily intentional; organizations get accustomed to using a kind of insider shorthand to communicate among themselves—no harm there. The problem occurs when internal jargon finds its way into external communication, which it inevitably and increasingly does. When this happens, companies are in effect talking to themselves in public.

Even something as seemingly straightforward as real estate can be made confusing. What exactly is a "Realtor"? How is that different from the terms "agent" and "broker"? How about "certified buyer representative"? Apparently there are at least eight types of real estate professionals: CBR, C-CREC, CEBA, CRP, CBA, CRS, ABR, and GRI. To most people, that's just alphabet soup.

Many insiders consider it a badge of honor to be able to speak jargon; they develop a sense of pride in being able to "talk the talk." For example, on Wall Street you'll hear people speak Internal Revenue Service tax code: 401(k)s, 403(b)s, 529s, and so on. Likewise, insurance companies talk about comprehensive coverage, umbrella policies, endorsements, riders, and deductibles. But insider terminology can mean something very different to an outsider: From the insurance company's perspective, the word "deductible" refers to the amount they deduct from what they pay you, but policyholders describe a deductible as the amount they pay before the insurance company starts paying. Pretty dramatic difference, no? The use of jargon is a prime example of lack of empathy—when you fail to consider the frame of reference in which your message will be received.

As a result, important messages can become "lost in translation," making it impossible to reach across lines, connect, and collaborate. In the midst of the September 11 tragedy, police lingo became a hindrance; emergency responders couldn't communicate because each had their own set of codes. Fortunately, many municipalities are dropping "10 code" in favor of "plain talk" radio transmissions.

Medical communication is particularly problematic, since even familiar words may be confusing when the context changes. How many of us have to stop and think about whether a first-degree or a third-degree burn is worse? Alan Alda, the well-known actor who is also a science buff, has challenged the scientific community to explain itself in ways that truly inform rather than substitute one mysterious topic for another. He cleverly cited his childhood question, "What is a flame?" and the unsatisfactory answer from a teacher, "Oxidation," as evidence of how many explanations are merely word substitutions that clarify nothing.[14] It is the job of professionals to think about their listeners and adjust their message, vocabulary, and level of detail accordingly.

With all of the forces and conditions fostering complexity, it might seem that the situation is irreversible—that once things become overly complicated, they can never go back to being simple. We have evidence to the contrary. The companies profiled in this book were once plagued by complexity but are now much simpler. Complex products have been replaced by more successful, simple ones. Complex documents have been replaced by easy-to-read communications. Complexity can be moved upstream, out of sight of the end user. Turning the key in a car's ignition is a simple task that masks a complicated set of underlying processes, and that is how all interactions should be for consumers.

Even the most complex situations can be made simple when there's a genuine desire and commitment to do it. Here's proof positive: The financial industry is awash in complexity and would have us believe that there is no way to conduct complex transactions and deals without voluminous fine print, jargon, and paperwork. And yet at the height of the financial crisis, when survival was at stake and there was no time for wasted words, government officials produced a TARP application that was a model of simplicity: *two pages long with four clear concise bullet points!* This document was then used by the Treasury to lend nearly $50 billion to the biggest banks.

The point here is that when there's a will to simplify, there is always a way. But the will must be there, and that means people must be convinced it is in their self-interest to simplify. One way to do that is to start by showing the power of simplicity as an untapped source of innovation. **Breakthrough simplicity** can help businesses, governments, and virtually any type of organization or endeavor to get better results—and sometimes even to break through to a higher level.

CHAPTER 2
·····················

Breakthrough Simplicity

A New Way of Thinking

HOW BANKS, AIRLINES—AND EVEN THE U.S.
GOVERNMENT—CAN INNOVATE BY OFFERING
LESS.

In a reclaimed warehouse space in Brooklyn, New York, Josh Reich, a young man with a flaming red beard, an Aussie accent, and the look of a mad scientist, is trying to reinvent banking.[1]

It's not hard to understand why: Banks are known for being faceless, impersonal, even antagonistic. Their talents seem to lie in complicating our lives, by way of maddening fees and baffling policies stipulating minimum balances and punitive penalties. And as Reich sees it, none of this is accidental.

"Banks want to keep people confused," he declared on a recent morning at the modest offices of his small start-up firm, humbly named Simple, where an empty Mac computer box serves as a makeshift coffee table. "They earn most of their money from fees and charges—and when you earn most of your money from people's mistakes, there's no incentive to change that. Instead, they foster that confusion."

> *"Any intelligent fool can make things bigger, more complex, and more violent. It takes a touch of genius—and a lot of courage—to move in the opposite direction."*
> —E. F. SCHUMACHER

Many of us might agree with that statement while also just accepting it—*Well, that's the way banks are.* But Reich envisions a different kind of banking, offering (as his company's name suggests) a radically simplified customer experience. Starting from scratch and unencumbered by traditional banking processes and systems, his mission is to get rid of the everyday hassles and annoyances of banking—which is why, for instance, Simple will charge no overdraft fees. This is a sharp contrast to the average listing of thirty-nine possible fees found at every major bank.

Beyond that, Reich has devised a high-tech banking system that manages the mundane account details most of us don't have time to attend to, such as keeping precise records of transactional details or moving money around so that it's always getting the best rate. At Simple, you only have one account, which is overseen by an algorithm-based system that makes constant investment and rebalancing decisions based on your stated financial needs and goals.

"One of our significant departures is that we think banks provide customers with *too many* choices," Reich says. "If you're like most people, you have six cards and accounts—a personal checking account, one you share with your spouse, a miles card, a debit card. But you have incomplete information and not enough time to manage all that." And you have one more thing: guilt. Reich is literally banking on the fact that people feel guilty about not paying enough attention to their everyday finances. Simple seeks to unburden them of that guilt.

The Simple system is almost entirely technology-based (you must have a smartphone to bank with them). To be a customer, you must also be willing to change your banking behavior—check writing is severely limited and paper rather than online account statements cost a hefty $20 per statement—so this new paradigm requires a change in consumer mindset. Reich also expects you to get answers online or through telephone self-service to the two most frequently asked questions: "Was my salary deposited?" and "What's my balance?" (A "Safe to Spend" tab is highlighted at the top of your mobile/web app, showing exactly how much you can safely spend at any given time.)

Reich won't have a bricks-and-mortar building with a vault full of cash; he's partnering with "back end" banks that will handle the money. What he's focused on is the front end: the interaction with customers, which will mostly be done digitally. This simplifies things not only for the customer but for Reich's company as well: It can focus efforts and resources entirely on the customer experience, ensuring that it's as user-friendly and accessible as possible.

Simple's website has an approachable, interactive design

with advanced search features and scrolling updates on all your financial info. (For example, it can tell you not only how much you spent at Target last Thursday, but *which register* rang you up.) Will customers really need all that metadata? They may— or they may just take comfort in knowing it's there in case they do need it. But either way, what separates this data from the kind of boilerplate fine print most banks foist upon us is that Simple's data is customized, and therefore potentially useful and relevant. Maps pop up alongside your list of transactions reminding you where you were when you made a purchase (see Figure 2.1).

While Reich believes that technology—if used in the right ways—can foster simplicity, he also understands there are times when the simplest way to solve a problem is via one human being talking to another. With most banks, when customers have a pressing question about their account, they call a phone number listed on their statement. Then they are shuttled through call centers and bounced to different attendants using separate computers (with each one asking you, yet again, for your account number). At each stop along the way, Reich notes, "they don't know who you are." Mindful of this, Simple has built its own software for running a call center that is designed to offer personalized one-to-one service. In fact, their call center is modeled on the best practices they identified when they visited the call center of the online shoe retailer Zappos. Reich is also trying to bring a human touch to other forms of communication with customers, including sending out personalized notes.

Figure 2.1   Simple.com home page.

When blogger Kristian Andersen signed up for an account recently, she got back a note addressed to her from an actual human being, who wrote, "I want to hear from you personally about what you want from a bank: your loves, hates, quibbles, desires, hopes and dreams regarding your financial life. Really: What's on your mind, and what are you hoping for from Bank-Simple?"

Andersen was duly impressed. "It conveyed empathy and

sincere interest in my opinions," she wrote on her blog, *KA+A*. "It was the first touchpoint, after signing up, and it beautifully reinforced the brand's promise of service and relationships." She added, "It's the little things, the touches that don't cost much, that make brands human and lovable."[2]

Time will tell if Reich's ambitious venture succeeds, but clearly he's on to something. Banks are failing their customers, and complexity is a big reason why. According to *Ad Age*, the Edelman Trust Barometer of 2010 found that "transparent and honest practices" was the most important standard of trust cited by 83 percent of respondents. Other surveys rank banks a dismal tenth out of thirteen business sectors on delivering the simplicity consumers seek. (Only utilities, insurance providers, and credit card companies managed to do worse.)[3]

We found that consumers are willing to pay a "simplicity premium" for things like cars, cell phones, train travel, and fitness services. In some cases, that premium rises to as high as 6 percent for brands offering a greater degree of simplicity (defined as ease of understanding, transparency, caring, innovation, and usefulness of communications). Extrapolated across all industries and sectors in the United States, that 4–6 percent could translate into $20 billion in revenue (see Figure 2.2).

In fact, it's hard to find any areas where people *don't* crave simplicity. Yet the products, services, and messages they're getting from business, healthcare providers, and government

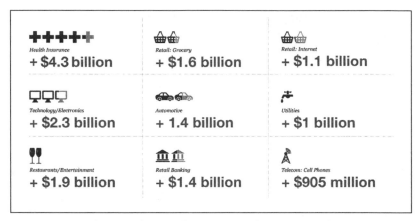

Figure 2.2   In the United States, businesses are leaving more than $20.1 billion on the table. Simplify and you shall receive. The health insurance industry could stand to capture the most, more than $4.3 billion to be precise, through clearer, understandable communications.

tend to have the opposite effect. Consider, for example, that half the gadgets purchased in the United States are returned in perfect working condition—primarily because people can't figure out how to use them.[4]

It may seem counterintuitive, but in a business environment that usually hypes "more, more, more," people increasingly are opting for *less*. They're responding to products with simpler features, and food with fewer ingredients. The ice cream maker Häagen-Dazs first observed this trend a few years ago when, as brand manager Ching-Yee Hu told *USA Today*, it began encountering focus group consumers who expressed a clear preference for food products with fewer ingredients. All of which made Hu wonder, "Why can't we bring ice cream down to the bare minimum?" What resulted was a new ice cream line called Five for its five ingredients—milk, cream, sugar, eggs, and vanilla bean. It was an immediate hit with consumers.[5]

Of course, people respond to the idea of a few ingredients because they assume that those five won't be dehydrated potato flakes, monosodium glutamate, whey solids, artificial coloring, and artificial flavoring. We can easily foresee a good idea (few ingredients) mutating when tainted by greed. Just as companies use simplicity as a come-on when the reality is much different, "few" ingredients shouldn't be hyped inappropriately when "few" doesn't deliver on purity and freshness.

It's not just consumer purchases, either; people not only want but *desperately need* simplicity in their medical services. And at the same time, they want and deserve it from their government too. Add it all up, and what you have is a wealth of possibilities for simplicity innovators like Josh Reich and others. Across a broad range of industries, encompassing all sorts of products and services, there is a growing need to rethink and reinvent by way of simplification.

> "Making the simple complicated is commonplace; making the complicated simple… that's creativity."
> —CHARLES MINGUS

This is the positive flip side of the worrisome crisis of complexity described in the preceding chapter: Within that crisis lies massive opportunity. In business, government, and healthcare, mounting complexity has erected barriers that make it harder for customers, patients, and citizens to get what they need. Simplicity can be the key to removing those barriers, which is not to suggest it's an easy fix.

Actually, what's required is not only creativity, but also an opportunistic mindset, a sensitivity to what people actually need (as opposed to what they're currently getting), and a willingness to cast off business-as-usual practices and approaches. We use the term **breakthrough simplicity** to describe an approach to innovation that is rooted in finding new ways to make *everything* simpler. It's a way of thinking that enables you to envision and pursue a wide range of possibilities that can lead to major breakthroughs.

This puts a fresh spin on "innovation"—that much-used, oft-misunderstood buzzword. There's a tendency to think of innovation as coming up with the latest gadget or adding new features onto existing ones. But the concept of breakthrough simplicity recognizes that today, the most powerful innovations don't manifest themselves as new bells and whistles. They take the form of better customer experiences (or patient experiences, or citizen experiences). And one of the best ways to improve any experience is to simplify it—to remove complications, unnecessary layers, hassles, or distractions, while focusing on the essence of what people want and need in that particular situation.

Breaking new ground via simplicity isn't so simple, of course. Part of what makes it hard is that within almost any industry or product category, complexity builds over time—and gradually comes to be accepted as an unavoidable part of doing business in that sector. It takes a maverick to come along and say, "Maybe things really *don't* have to be so complicated." This was the case with Southwest Airlines. Four decades ago, Southwest was looking for an opening in the airline business, which was crowded, chaotic, and complex even back then. At the time Southwest was first taking wing, it was assumed that running an airline meant dealing with all manner of cost inefficiencies and inherent complexities, from maintaining a large and diverse fleet of planes to the logistics of serving dinner to each passenger. It seemed there was just no way around these everyday hassles of running an airline—until Southwest proved otherwise.

Instead of having its fleet stocked with various types of planes, Southwest opted for a one-plane-fits-all approach by flying only Boeing 737s. And while other airlines had grown used to a multistop hub-and-spoke system to get passengers to their destinations, Southwest made the bold decision to focus on direct nonstop flights. On those flights, they would serve snacks rather than full meals. This streamlining of the business model created tremendous efficiencies for Southwest, saving money on plane maintenance, food, and cleaning costs, while also ensuring that its planes spent more time aloft and less on the ground. As Portfolio.com noted, the airline "keeps things simple and consistent, which drives costs down" and "maximizes productive assets."[6]

Of course, all that streamlining could have diminished the

customer experience, but Southwest turned it into a positive by focusing on simple, basic benefits that mattered a lot to its customers. It used the cost savings to offer lower fares; it nixed the annoying hidden fees and surcharges that other airlines levy on customers; it doesn't charge for baggage; it has fewer flight delays than other airlines, in part because of its point-to-point flying system.

And while it cut back on food, Southwest amped up the in-flight experience by encouraging pilots and attendants to banter and joke with passengers—which they have become known for doing with gusto. The overall business results are well documented: Southwest has been one of the few consistently profitable airlines over the past three decades.

But the larger point proved by Southwest is that no industry or category of business, regardless of how inherently complex it may be, is beyond simplification. In fact, the more complex an industry is, and the more complicated a particular product or service within that industry may be, the more opportunities there are for simplification—and the more it will tend to be valued and appreciated by customers.

Simplicity as a luxury

Offering simplicity within a complex domain is likely to be so appreciated and valued by customers that it ends up being perceived as a luxury. That may surprise some marketers who make the common mistake of thinking that in order to position a brand as a "luxury" alternative, you must provide customers with more features, perks, and options; luxury, in this context, is equated with "excess." But we've found that consumers of luxury goods have even *less* time and desire than most to wade through choices. One way to carve out a luxury niche is by simplifying—by making it easier for customers to use a product or service without having to waste time thinking about it or sorting through too many options. The key, however, is to make the right high-quality choices for these customers—and then make sure they understand that what you're providing is a simple solution that has considered their needs, made the right choices for them, and eliminated headaches and potential problems.

We learned this lesson early on in one of our first experiences working in the insurance industry. One doesn't often think of insurance as a glamorous, luxurious business. But the creation of a unique insurance policy called Masterpiece, which we helped design for Chubb Insurance, was a simplicity breakthrough within the industry. Chubb already held a prominent place in the commercial insurance market, but in the mid-1980s the company responded to requests from the owners and executives of the businesses it insured by offering personal coverage. These individuals typically were quite affluent and required a mix and match of coverage for valuable articles (such as jewelry and art collections), watercraft (yachts), homes (several), and cars (luxury models).

Masterpiece eschewed the typical insurance policy jargon

in favor of simple, plain English that a policyholder could read from cover to cover and understand. This meant that they abandoned the ISO industry-standard forms (a path of least resistance for many insurers since by using the standard they know that they are in compliance with state regulations even if those regulations aren't particularly comprehensible for policy-holders). They did this to better reflect how they actually conduct their business and handle claims.

Masterpiece was also a fully customizable policy. The possible combinations of coverage were numerous, yet a library of modular text read seamlessly when printed as a continuous flow. The beauty of the policy stemmed from the fact that clarity and transparency are the bedrock of the Chubb brand. Chubb takes the approach of telling policyholders what is excluded, and if something is *not specifically excluded*, it is covered. By sending an appraiser to every home to set the replacement cost value before insuring it and giving the actual replacement cost if they estimate incorrectly, the effect is a "hassle-free" claims experience.

> Having a Masterpiece policy has become a status symbol. Sixty percent of the Forbes 400 wealthiest people in the United States and half of Fortune 500 CEOs have Chubb personal insurance.

The policy was not only simple for the customer to read, but it was also designed to be easier and faster for Chubb to underwrite and approve. This meant that 95 percent of policies and 97 percent of endorsements could be out the door within seven days, in an industry that typically measures turnaround in weeks. That put more money in Chubb's pocket, because insurance companies that turn around policies faster can nab more customers; it's an early-bird-gets-the-worm business. And at the same time, Chubb could command a higher "luxury" premium on the policy, which people would pay because there was no guesswork about coverage and no hassles when a claim was filed.

Customizing content, as Chubb did with Masterpiece, is a form of simplicity because it involves winnowing information and increasing relevancy. By doing so, a company can save customers time and build their trust. Even the largest company can achieve the illusion that it is speaking to you and only you. Why don't more companies take this approach? Why don't they take the time and effort to customize and simplify their offerings?

One reason is that consumers historically have not been vocal about demanding simplicity, which has caused companies to be complacent about it. Companies haven't invested the time and effort in thinking about simplification, or in reforming entrenched practices that foster complexity. They have underserved their customers in this area, because it seemed they could get away with it.

But that's changing. Today, it's clear that most people— more than 80 percent—are looking for ways to simplify their lives.[7] Some of this is undoubtedly a reaction to a world that's getting more fast-paced, hyperconnected, and overloaded with information, choices, and distractions.

> The MS & L Worldwide Global Values Study, conducted by Roper in 2008 with six thousand people worldwide, found that 72 percent of U.S. consumers want companies to be more transparent. The study concluded that transparency in business today "is not an option. It's a necessity."

The interesting thing is that this craving for simplicity spans demographic groups. One might tend to assume that older consumers would be most resistant to growing complexity—and it's true, there is a tremendous market opportunity out there in simplifying things for the multitudes of aging baby boomers. But it may surprise some to learn that this issue resonates just as strongly with younger consumers.

According to a recent survey by the research firm Outlaw Consulting, the youngest wave of Generation Y consumers (those aged twenty-one to twenty-seven) responds very positively to brands that communicate with them in a "straightforward and stripped-down way, use plain packaging, and avoid excess," in the words of Outlaw Consulting analyst Holly Brickley. The respondents cited a number of companies as admirable models of simplicity, including Apple, Trader Joe's, JetBlue, and In-N-Out Burger (known for its limited, no-frills burger menu). One of the qualities these younger respondents associate with simplicity is authenticity—that is, "keeping it simple" is tantamount to "keeping it real."[8]

Many brands these days would kill to be thought of by younger consumers as "real" and "authentic," yet they fail to recognize that simplicity—in their products, packaging, and messaging—is one of the most important ways to convey this quality. That failure is on full display in advertising. An Adweek/Harris Poll noted that three-quarters of Americans have found a commercial on TV confusing.[9] On a more consistent basis, 21 percent often find that commercials lack clarity.

When we talk about breakthrough simplicity, we mean an interaction that cuts through the clutter. This is a standard that should be applied to everything a company puts out into the world, from the product to the ads down to the smallest piece of correspondence: It should do its job quickly, clearly, simply. People just don't have the time or the interest to wade through corporate rhetoric and jargon to figure out what you're trying to tell them. Through clarity of thought and presentation, it's possible for a business to rise above the cacophony of today's marketplace.

Because simplification can impact business on numerous levels, it is imperative that it be championed from on high. When it is, simplicity encourages honesty, since it's hard to hoodwink customers if your communications are straightforward and your practices are transparent. It provides efficiencies to businesses that become easier to manage thanks to focused, clear strategies and streamlined approaches. It can also foster an internal corporate clarity—helping people within the company to better understand what they're trying to achieve and, perhaps, why they got into the business in the first place. And last and foremost—getting back to what matters most in business—simplicity sells.

People have needs that transcend issues of profitability and market share. So it's important to point out that simplicity not only sells, it can save—as in save lives. One of the areas we've found to be most ripe for reinvention through simplicity is healthcare. Everyone has an interest in seeing innovation and improvement in patient care. And if you've been to a hospital recently—or even just had a conversation with your doctor— you know that the levels of complexity in this domain can be head-spinning. When we talk about the healthcare industry embracing simplicity, it isn't just a business imperative; it's a moral one as well. This may be the reason why some medical professionals are already on the front lines of the war against complexity, where they're providing valuable lessons on how to gain ground.

There aren't many places more chaotic than a hospital, which makes it an ideal lab to test simplification strategies. And these days, medical centers such as the Mayo Clinic, Kaiser

Permanente, and Cleveland Clinic are among a number of pioneers that are experimenting with ways to simplify the following:

The Interaction Between Nurses

Shift changes in hospitals create disruptions in the continuity of patient care, but at Kaiser Permanente the development of a simple protocol requiring nurses on changing shifts to exchange information with each other at the patient's bedside—with the patient encouraged to participate—has lessened communication breakdowns.[10]

The Way Surgeons Keep Track of What Needs to Be Done Next

By adapting airplane checklists first devised by Boeing, a number of hospitals are now using a checklist approach to make sure that during surgery there is a specific, brief set of questions and procedures to follow at all times.

The Menu of Services Offered by Hospitals

Just as retailers are seeing the benefits of narrowing their focus, hospitals are doing likewise—opting for more specialization in, for example, one type of surgery. You need an elbow fixed, you go here; need a heart mended, you go there.

Of course, the "complications" associated with medical treatment don't end when you leave the hospital—in fact, that's when things can get more confusing. Patients are suddenly on their own, with regimens to follow, prescriptions to fill, and voluminous bills to pay. Each of those steps can be simplified, and some innovators are showing how. Already there is a movement under way, led by people working at medical centers around the country, to make hospital bills less complicated and even get hospitals to explain costs better in advance, during check-in. Meanwhile, the Walgreens drugstore chain is seizing an opportunity by addressing the need to make sure that discharged patients promptly get their prescriptions filled (something that a surprising number of them fail to do); the retailer recently announced a new service that initiates the process of filling prescriptions at the hospital bedside, *before* the patient is discharged.

"Let me be clear…"

If there's any area that offers even more potential for reinvention than healthcare, it's government. Believe it or not, the U.S. government was once a model of simplicity—consider, for instance, that it was founded on the basis of a document that was a mere six pages long. But it's been a long time since that kind of brevity and simplicity has been on display in Washington.

Various administrations over the past forty years have sought to simplify government, and some have even taken modest steps toward that goal, the most recent being the Obama administration—which came in promising a new era of transparency and simplicity in government. The financial crisis had brought trust in business and government to new lows, and as President Obama took office in early 2009, our own surveys showed that 79 percent of Americans wanted the president to "mandate that clarity, transparency and plain-English be a requirement for every new law, regulation and policy."[11]

Obama certainly seemed to be the right man for the job: an agent of change, an excellent communicator, and a man known for often starting sentences with the phrase, "Let me be clear." On his very first day in office, Obama issued a memo calling for transparency in government. "Government should be participatory," the memo stated. "Public engagement enhances the government's effectiveness and improves the quality of its decisions."[12] A year later, he signed the Plain Writing Act of 2010, requiring that government documents be in language that's "clear, concise, and well-organized."

That said, by 2011 there was a sense of missed opportunity in Obama's efforts to simplify and clarify government. In a ForeSee Results survey, Americans gave the White House low marks—a score of 46 out of a possible 100—on attempts to be transparent about what the West Wing was doing. (Congress rated even lower, at 37.)[13] Meanwhile, according to our own survey, two-thirds of Americans (65 percent) felt that the U.S. government wasn't doing a good job of communicating what benefits and services its agencies provide to citizens.

The Obama administration has asserted that it is the most transparent administration ever, and in terms of "full disclosure," that's probably true: No previous government has put so much information out there on the Internet (see Figure 2.3). But if we use the "organized disclosure" standard for transparency, the Obama administration comes up short. If there's a lesson here, it's that simplification requires more than good intentions and first steps. While the Obama administration

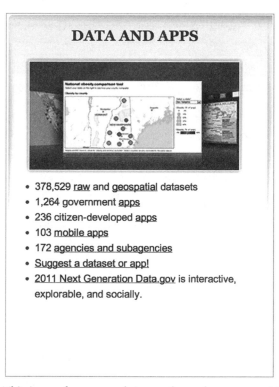

Figure 2.3   This image from www.data.gov shows the amount of info the U.S. government is making available on its website: access to hundreds of agencies, thousands of apps, hundreds of thousands of datasets.

started off in the right direction by making more government information directly available to the public, that data needed to be organized, written, and designed to facilitate readability. Instead, the government simply shoveled massive amounts of data onto sites like Recovery.gov, Data.gov, and USAspending .gov. It remains impenetrable to the average citizen, who still can't figure out where his or her tax dollar is going.

Interestingly, the communication opportunity that was squandered by the data-dumping government has been seized upon by a number of private individuals and businesses, who've taken that raw data and turned it into smartphone apps and websites that provide people with useful information on everything from public transit schedules to weather forecasts. That's progress of a sort, and it certainly couldn't have happened if the government hadn't released the data. But by letting others filter and shape the data, the government is missing out on a chance to connect directly with citizens (which was what Obama talked about in that first-day memo).

For a long time it has been assumed that government is just too big and complex to simplify—that it is too mired in bureaucracy and too bound up in arcane regulations and laws that are centuries old.

There are some practical ways to begin to break the government's legal and bureaucratic logjam. The introduction of the short-form 1040EZ tax return in 1980 was a radical innovation:

Tiered forms, tailored to reflect the reality that some taxpayers have little more than salary to report, rescued many from the maze of forms and instructions and saved millions of hours of people's time. The IRS, to its credit, followed that up a decade and a half later by offering the option to file the 1040EZ by phone, which saved a few million more hours. (A similar option offered to business tax filers in 1998 provided an even bigger time-saving benefit.)

In 1999, however, the trail of simplification grew cold. That year, the federal paperwork burden had one of its biggest one-year increases ever, and 90 percent of the increase was attributable to the IRS. To look at this opportunistically, this means there's a lot of fat there for the trimming—and lately, many on all sides of the political spectrum have begun to wave their cleavers.

The movement to simplify the tax code probably has as much momentum now as it has had in years. Everyone from political candidates to the IRS's own taxpayer advocate, Nina E. Olson, is putting forth ideas and proposals for how to rewrite and simplify the system. One suggested solution is a progressive flat tax—a system with just a few tax rates. That type of solution attempts to address the numerous deductions, exemptions, and exceptions shown in the following chart. Attempts to

"Our democracy is now run by dead people."

—PHILIP K. HOWARD, FOUNDER OF COMMON GOOD, COMMENTING ON THE RESTRICTIONS IMPOSED BY LAWS AND REGULATIONS WRITTEN DECADES OR EVEN CENTURIES AGO reform the system would have to figure out how to eliminate or at least distill these infinite variables, without undermining the fairness and integrity of the tax system. It's a difficult but worthwhile challenge. Preparing tax returns would automatically become simpler because the number of entries on the forms would be radically reduced.

This is just one example of how the complexity that is rife within government offers a potentially potent political opportunity for anyone willing to take a stand for simplicity. In fact,

Factors That Complicate Income Tax

Type of Income	Who Earned It?	How Much?	Does It All Count?
Wages	Married	Different rates for different levels of income (tax brackets)	Deductions
Capital gains, interest, dividends	Single		Exemptions
Royalties, rental income	Same-sex partners		Credits
	Unmarried members of same household		
	Older (above age sixty-five)		
	Blind, disabled		
	Parents		

Even the terms "deductions," "exemptions," and "credits" are indistinguishable to many taxpayers.

we've been surprised that the political candidates, from either or both parties, haven't staked out a stronger position on making government more accessible to citizens. A call for clarity would be a powerful message that would likely resonate with voters. But the candidate who took that stand, if elected, would have to tackle the problem with more than vague promises and voluminous data dumps. They'd have to approach it with what we call a mindset and a systematic approach geared toward simplification.

Of course, there is no magical five- or six-step formula for simplification. We've seen far too many would-be simplifiers try to employ Six Sigma processes and data-driven testing to battle complexity. They time customer service calls to hundredths of a second and monitor mouse clicks by the millions, to no avail. We've seen businesses try to automate their way to simplicity—as in the hotel that uses technology to handle everything from check-in to wake-up calls, the result being that there is no human contact and no opportunity to ask that individualized, idiosyncratic question the machine can't answer.

Simplification requires a thorough and pervasive commitment by an organization to **empathize, distill,** and **clarify** (see Figure 2.4).

It requires us to have the discipline to boil down to its essence what we're offering or communicating. It's also about shaping, filtering, purifying, and customizing whatever is being

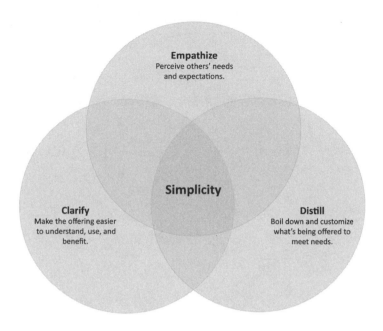

Figure 2.4

offered to people so that it best meets their needs and expectations. It demands that we strive for clarity, through the use of
both plain language and design. But it all starts, as we'll see in
the next chapter, with empathy—with a willingness and ability to look at a contract, application, product, or service with a
sense of the person on the other end. To make something simple, you must care enough to consider people's circumstances,
needs, and expectations—and then respond to them.

PART II

The Three Principles of Simplicity

CHAPTER 3

······················

Empathize

SIMPLICITY IS ABOUT SHORTENING THE
DISTANCE BETWEEN COMPANY AND CUSTOMER;
HOSPITAL AND PATIENT; GOVERNMENT AND
CITIZEN. IT ALL STARTS WITH UNDERSTANDING
THE CIRCUMSTANCES AND NEEDS OF OTHERS.

"Am I in a hospital—or a luxury hotel?" You may find yourself asking that question if you ever visit Cleveland Clinic.

With bright and airy atriums, classical music playing, paintings and sculptures all around, and a red-jacketed reception staff, the atmosphere at the hospital's main campus is a soothing alternative to the typically chaotic, uninviting hospital environment. You won't see patients on gurneys; they're transported through the hospital using service elevators that are removed from public view (because, frankly, no one in that situation wants to be on display, and no one visiting needs to see it). The hospital's extensive security—its campus is eighteen

> *"A man, to be greatly good, must imagine intensely and comprehensively; he must put himself in the place of another and of many others; the pains and pleasures of his species must become his own."*
> —PERCY BYSSHE SHELLEY

times safer than the surrounding community—is also well hidden. At Cleveland Clinic, there is plenty of complexity all around, but you just can't see it. It has been moved out of the way.[1]

As we walked through the clinic—with some guidance provided by a touchscreen wayfinding avatar named Maria who was happy to print directions for us—we noticed other small differences. The place even smells pleasant; the air is fresh, without the stale antiseptic tinge that is the aromatic mask of most hospitals.

But the difference goes beyond atmosphere—it resides in the many small details of the patient experience. Everything from the way doctors talk to patients (in plain English, and with a willingness to answer questions until there are none left), to the hospital gowns (designed by Diane von Furstenberg to combine ease of access with a touch of dignity), to the clear, concise bills you receive after checking out—all of it reflects a commitment to simplifying the interaction between a human being and a large, complex medical establishment.

You might say that Cleveland Clinic is transitioning from being in the *hospital* business to the *hospitality* business. Why would it opt to do that? Well, in recent years, top hospitals have been competing to attract patients, including out-of-towners. Initially, they tried to woo these prospects with ads touting hospital rankings for various specialized services and access to high-tech equipment. The message was: *It's worth traveling to the best hospital.*

Trouble is, most patients are hard pressed to define what makes a hospital the "best," until they start doing some informal research: talking to friends of friends, going on patient websites, putting out feelers on Facebook. That's when they begin to learn how patients who've been to a particular hospital actually feel about it. And that's where the soft, nebulous phenomenon of "patient experience" can be more important than numerical rankings or top-notch medical equipment.

What makes the biggest impression on people during their stay in a hospital? As Cleveland Clinic learned, it's the small details: how long it takes a nurse to answer the call bell, the availability of food on request, whether staff members follow the "10-4" rule ("when ten feet away from a patient, smile and make eye contact; when four feet away, address the patient"). Of course, getting out of the place alive and healthy is paramount, but that's viewed as table stakes—patients *expect* the operation or procedure to be successful. What they remember (and talk about to others) are all those casual human exchanges that occur during the stay.

And there are *a lot* of those. When Cleveland Clinic's "chief experience officer," Dr. James Merlino, first tried to take stock of the many interactions someone typically has at the hospital, "the epiphany was that a hundred people control what that experience is going to be by the time the patient leaves." All of which meant Cleveland Clinic was dealing with a complex challenge: How do you orchestrate that many interactions? And how do you know if you're doing it right?

The hospital's leaders figured it couldn't be done via halfway measures. So a complete organizational overhaul took place four years ago, with Merlino installed to oversee a newly created "Office of Patient Experience." "We made patient experience an executive priority," Merlino says.

Nearly forty thousand employees were trained in forty days—from custodians to neurosurgeons—to take on the title of "caregiver" and become patient-focused. Merlino points out that the only way to improve all those staff/patient interactions was to have employees "take ownership" of their small part of the patient experience—even parking lot attendants and food court workers who were technically not employees of the hospital. Together, the hospital's leaders and staff grappled with basic questions such as, "What does patient experience mean?" and developed policies and practices for how to address patients or answer questions.

One priority was to make sure that patients—who often are overwhelmed at hospitals by medical jargon and complicated instructions—could understand what they're being told. A team of "healthcare literacy" experts now coaches staff and reviews all printed matter for patients. Nurses talk more with patients as part of their hourly rounding. Doctors are expected to explain procedures clearly and field all questions. And patients, too, are urged to communicate more: Merlino says, "We tell patients, 'You're 50 percent of the partnership in your care—you can help us by telling us what's working or not.'"

One of the keys to the success of this transformation is the use of extensive feedback. The hospital gathers lots of it from patients and doesn't hold back in sharing it with even the most esteemed surgeons—who can actually see how their communication skills have been graded by patients (and verbatim complaints are shared, too). All that data is fed into sophisticated patient experience "dashboards" so that hospital leaders can monitor, in real time, survey results and feedback trends.

Virtually every point of contact with patients has been cleaned up and simplified. It starts with the first call to the hospital; there's just one number to call and anyone can get a same-day appointment if they request it (highly unusual for a clinic of this size). And it ends with post-visit bills: They still can hurt, but Cleveland Clinic tries to soften the blow by starting the billing process with a personalized thank-you note and an explanation of "what you can expect" in terms of insurance copayments (which are automatically credited) and follow-up statements.

Early on, the clinic recognized that "a great experience for the staff makes for a great experience for patients." One program that meets employee needs is "Code Lavender." When a patient dies and an employee found it to be a particularly traumatic event, the employee can request special counseling. (As part of this, they're given a lavender wristband that alerts other staff to be sensitive in dealing with them.) During lighter periods, the clinic also offers nurses three-day, thirteen-hour shifts (instead of five-day, eight-hour shifts) so they have more free time.

The clinic knows that empathy is too often lacking among people coming out of med school. Indeed, Deirdre Mylod, PhD, a healthcare consultant with Press Ganey (which specializes in customer experience), reports that "research suggests empathy actually *decreases* in med students and residents during medical training."[2] With this in mind, Cleveland Clinic uses the "Previsor" test (a personality assessment screener) to hire based on attitude, not just skill.

What's the result of all this? The business benefits for Cleveland Clinic are many, not only in terms of attracting more patients but increasing per-patient revenues. Efforts such as simplifying and clarifying the hospital bill sharply improve the likelihood of prompt payment (which can generate as much as $1 million a month in revenue increase). But there are other benefits that transcend bottom-line concerns: Patients who are more informed and engaged in their treatment at the hospital are more likely to respond to treatment and have a better recovery. They're also more apt to go out there and spread the word about which hospital is the best.

For Cleveland Clinic, the revolutionary "patients first" movement is still in its nascent stages. But the medical care industry—including top-tier competitors like the Mayo Clinic—is watching closely and developing other similar initiatives. What's becoming clear to many on the front lines of this movement is that a hospital can have the best doctors and the most cutting-edge technology, but it's not enough. Today's caregivers must *care* in a whole new way, in being willing and able to see things from the patient's perspective. To improve the hospital experience, they must empathize with people's particular situations, concerns, needs, and expectations. It's no longer just about having the top heart specialists—now the hospital itself must have a heart.

To some extent, *all* companies today are in the "experience" business. How do you manage and improve customer experience when every customer is unique and some interactions are life-changing while others are forgotten in an instant?

Think about why many customer experiences come up short: It's because customers are not getting what they expect or what they need from a product, service, or interaction with a company. Many things can get in the way of satisfaction—miscommunication, underperformance, complications, confusion—and as they do, the distance between company and customer grows. Simplicity is about removing those barriers and shortening that distance.

It's also about helping business to get in touch with the reality of people's situations and needs. Countless products, instructions, and services are made unnecessarily difficult because real-world considerations were overlooked. We've all asked the questions, "Who designs these things?!" or "Who wrote this?!" Usually, it's as we're struggling with impenetrable packaging or trying to turn off an exasperating alarm. Similarly, the more luxurious your car, the more likely its owner's manual will fill your entire glove compartment, and you still won't be able to reset the clock. Despite the time, money, and attention paid to the design of your owner's manual, it is still useless when you have a problem on the road.

We call it the "design-in-a-vacuum phenomenon," and it explains a lot of the world we live in, like how microscopically sized drug instructions evolved. The labels that wrap around over-the-counter medication bottles, although they are marvels of printing technology, now unfurl with type so small that even those in the best of health can't read them.

Every day throughout corporate America, task forces examine processes, streamline interfaces, and redesign documents with an eye toward "simplifying" them. Why then does complexity still abound whether you are booking a flight, buying a vacuum cleaner, or calling a bank? Why is it always a case of retrofitting? Why is it so rare for a product or service to be launched with simplicity baked into it?

We maintain the missing ingredient is…(drum roll)… EMPATHY.

By empathizing, we mean imagining the context in which someone will buy, read, or use the product or service you're offering, then designing that offering to reflect those needs first and foremost. Since simplicity is the takeaway experience of an interaction, it follows that the creator of the experience must "get inside the head" of the recipient to anticipate how the interaction will be perceived.

Here's a dramatic example of what we're talking about: Imagine you're in a twenty-fifth-floor hotel room, and the fire alarm goes off in the middle of the night. You study the "You Are Here" diagram on the back of the door to find out where the nearest exit is. In that context, it looks more like a maze than an escape map. Why isn't it clearer, easier to figure out quickly? Because those safety instructions were developed in an entirely different context—in relaxed conditions, with plenty of light and time to study the instructions and decipher them. The instructions were created without empathy.

Try the same exercise when you are settling in for your next airplane ride and examine the safety card in the seatback. You'll realize that it too may have seemed fine when it was created in an office but now is unintelligible in a real-world setting.

The only meaningful measure of the success of this document is to test it in a way that lets you evaluate both perception and comprehension in the proper context. You'd want to hand it out on several flights and get reactions from a range of passengers who are typical of any flight—elderly, children flying alone, jaded road warriors, fearful first-time flyers, and so on. Give them only a limited amount of time to interact with the card—after all, you don't get to study before a sudden emergency. Ask them how they interpret the icons, what their eyes were drawn to first, which items seemed superfluous, and so forth.

Ford Motor Co. seemed to find this out the hard way when it announced in November 2011 that it was sending customers who'd bought vehicles equipped with a digital dashboard control system, called MyFord Touch, a free upgrade following complaints about the system's appearance and operation. Using a touchscreen in a moving vehicle is a far cry from studying it in the boardroom. *The upgrade relies on a four-quadrant screen layout so that without looking at the screen the driver will easily learn and remember where commands are located: upper left, lower right, and so on.*

We know—talking about empathy in a business context sounds so . . . *soft*. It evokes a certain sentiment not usually associated with corporate America or profitability. But it's important to understand that empathy is not the same as sympathy.

We definitely don't suggest that you turn your call center into a therapy help line, or that you internalize your customers' breakups, unemployment, or hatred of in-laws. We don't suggest you *sympathize* with a customer's plight, but that you *empathize* with their circumstances to gain insight into the customer perspective.

Of course, the standard definition of empathy generally refers to the understanding of another's *feelings*. What we are proposing is an emphasis on the understanding of another's *thought processes*, *decision-making strategies*, and *attention spans*.

For simplification to be effective, one must take into account everything that may affect the user's rational processing. So in circumstances where emotion is likely to overwhelm rational decision making—for instance, medical emergencies, divorce settlements, home purchases, estate planning—then it is equally critical to empathize with a person's emotional state. Physical distress, enormity of impact, and urgency are filters through which the essential information must be sifted.

Beyond considering real-world needs, successful simplifiers also cater to customer wants (for example, by pointing out on my bill that I might benefit from a different calling plan), and build in flexibility to avoid pigeonholing customers (why not let me choose what day of the month I pay my mortgage?). Smart companies ask customers what their preferences are and build a connection. Edward Jones, an investment firm, seized on this opportunity intelligently when it offered investors three levels of detail for investment performance reports. Customizing content is a powerful way to establish an enduring bond.

By incorporating these practices, empathetic design can boost sales and increase customer loyalty by making products and services designed specifically for each individual customer. The result is a closing of the gap between customer expectations and what a company actually delivers.

Current evidence suggests that the gap between what customers expect and what companies deliver has become a chasm. One recent Customer Care Alliance study found that 70 percent of American consumers have had a bad customer service experience in the past year that left them "upset" or "extremely upset."[3] The web publication *TechCrunch* reports that 82 percent of Americans say they've stopped doing business with companies because of poor service.[4]

The Customer Care Alliance study found that an "enraged consumer" is highly likely to tell friends and family about the bad experience—and not just a few, but typically about eighteen other people. But that's nothing compared to the influence exerted when a person blogs about the experience (and creates a funny chart, which then ends up in a book). Unhappy customers have always been a nightmare for companies, but never more so than in the age of social media, where outraged complaints and grievances can go viral.

On some level, companies understand that they must make customers happy. But there's a tendency in business to think the relationship with customers revolves entirely around the product—make a good widget, and the rest is mere window dressing. However, people are unpredictable and emotional creatures. Often the product becomes incidental, and seemingly small interactions—the way a salesperson answered a question or the tone of a letter sent by the company—become the most memorable aspects of the customer/company relationship.

Daniel Oppenheimer, professor of psychology at Princeton University, says that in dealings with businesses, it's often the emotional reactions that persist. "If a company treats you poorly, you may not remember the specifics of the incident, but it will leave a sour taste in your mouth whenever you think about that company." Oppenheimer notes that a positive association also can have remarkable lasting power.[5]

A *Fast Company* article declared that "For Brands, Being Human Is the New Black," making the point that brands are increasingly gaining traction by embracing qualities like honesty, kindness, and having a sense of humor about themselves. "Today, brands are taking on more and more human-like traits," noted the IDEO communications designer Elle Luna.[6]

Customers are fed up with bureaucracies that inundate us with generic and impersonal information, don't take our calls, create convoluted procedures, request too many signatures, provide baffling instructions, erect barriers of legalese, and find a thousand other ways to distance themselves from us.

As consumers, we experience these frustrations on a daily basis, so much so that it's pleasantly surprising—and memorable—when we happen upon a different kind of interaction.

Our first encounter with ING Direct USA, an online bank, was one of those rare experiences.[7] Seeking only to park some cash in an easily accessible savings account that offered the highest return, we didn't expect much in the way of customer service. But it soon became clear that ING paid attention to the details that improve customer experience. It began with their "opt-in" privacy policy, meaning they wouldn't share your personal information unless you want them to. Every other financial services company does the opposite: Unless you tell them *not* to (often a laborious process in itself), they and their corporate cousins, aunts, and uncles use your data to inundate you with offers of products and services.

When ING sent a letter confirming a PIN number change, it sounded like it was written by a person, not a computer, closing with the line, "If it is correct, then all you have to do is have a great day." Then there was the account statement: Rather than hide customer service phone numbers, the bill displayed them prominently across the bottom of the page, and the first choice is, "To speak to a real person." What—no phone tree?! Upon calling, we spoke to not only a real person, but one in the United States; it turns out ING doesn't outsource its customer service function to cheap-labor markets. This attention to detail simplifies the customer experience by anticipating customers' concerns and answering their questions before they ask them.

We were impressed enough to seek out Arkadi Kuhlmann, the chairman and CEO of ING Direct USA, to learn more, and we discovered that ING's straightforward correspondence was a reflection of a larger simplification philosophy. Kuhlmann believes there is too much clutter and noise in our lives, as evidenced by the clamor surrounding seven thousand banks. Kuhlmann also explained that simplicity and clarity help companies be more authentic and gain an edge in the marketplace. And if that weren't reason enough, there are social virtues: "Simplicity and clarity is good for American society, not just good business sense. It makes us more productive."

A big problem in business today, Kuhlmann maintains, is that too many companies "focus on short-term shareholder value, instead of maximizing the number of loyal customers and recognizing their long-term potential." This leads to various unsavory practices, like hitting customers with hidden fees.

Kuhlmann wanted to appeal to "protest customers" who are rebelling against bank fees, so the lack of fees became a prominent feature in all the company's communications. "Know thy audience" has become a platitude, yet in this case it's the key to fine-tuning ING Direct's marketing message and emphasizing the low-fee approach across all product lines, from savings accounts to mutual funds. The company designed its offerings with other ease-of-use conveniences, too: no minimum balance on savings, for instance, as well as a feature that lets customers easily create sub-accounts for specific purposes like vacations, with money transferred automatically from other accounts. ING Direct even simplified its mortgages, normally a hornet's nest of confusion and gobbledygook. The company reengineered the process to quickly approve customers and then backtrack to verify the supplied information, creating a nearly paperless transaction with automated underwriting. By simplifying its suite of products, ING Direct also distinguished its brand from the big banks that have created a plethora of account types. While empathetic to the needs of customers, it is also smart business.

In terms of how customers felt about ING, the proof is in the numbers: ING Bank's customer satisfaction rates have been as high as 98 percent. And in a PricewaterhouseCoopers ranking of the world's most respected companies, ING Direct was one of the seven financial names that CEOs respect for their integrity. Even the company's customer survey mechanism is unusually transparent: They solicit customer feedback on their website and *post the results*. The polling is also ongoing— Kuhlmann views it as an early warning system instead of a diagnostic tool to be used after trouble has begun.

Another indication that ING Direct has the right idea: When Capital One announced its acquisition of ING Direct USA in 2011, ING's faithful customers were so concerned about losing a "friend" that they went online and wrote enough emotional letters that the *New York Times* ran a story on it.[8] If your company were acquired by someone, would your customers be writing angst-filled letters? All of this will hopefully convince Capital One that not only shouldn't they mess with ING's policies—they should *learn* from them.

The main point ING Direct teaches us is that removing the often small yet significant barriers that create a sense of separation between you and your customers—everything from fees to form letters to no-money-back policies—changes the whole customer experience. Get rid of those barriers and you may lose a nickel or dime here and there—but you'll begin to close the "gap" and thereby cause your brand to be nearer and dearer to customers, who'll espouse your virtues and remain loyal.

But how do you figure out what those barriers are? How do you know what, exactly, is causing problems and complexity for your customers?

Companies often claim to "understand their customer"—

they conduct surveys, track us online, compile databases, and run focus groups (notoriously bad predictors of actual consumer behavior). But all the cold, hard data in the world isn't going to improve the customer experience unless you act on it with imagination and empathy. You can try to aid your imagination in various ways, making use of research, observation, ethnography, and so on, but what matters more than the tools per se is the level of commitment to empathy. Companies that place it at the highest level of importance tend to produce better, simpler, more pleasing customer experiences.

When it comes to empathy, context is everything. And sometimes the only way to fully understand context is to physically place yourself in it. When the design firm IDEO, known for its empathic research techniques, was working with a hospital on trying to simplify and improve patient experience, some of the firm's designers actually crawled into hospital beds to see things from the patient's perspective. Among other discoveries, they realized that patients spend a lot of time staring at the ceiling, which led to recommendations to decorate ceiling space or, better yet, use it to post patient information.[9]

Most companies never get out of their own corporate bubble. While empathy involves imagination, real-life experience can be a tool to exercise the imagination and gain insights. This phenomenon is captured in the popular reality TV series *Undercover Boss*, where a CEO goes to work incognito in various parts of his or her company to find out what it's like on the front lines. It enables them to empathize through direct experience rather than intellectual knowledge of the business. When CEO Ronald Croatti of UniFirst, a leading provider of uniforms, went undercover in his company, he acted upon the insights he gained and changed several processes. When he had great difficulty buttoning the collars of wet shirts prior to pressing them, he commissioned a test of snaps as a replacement for buttons to speed up the pressing line, a simpler task leading to greater productivity.

Ethnographic research—which is generally conducted through the participatory observation of a group of people—is useful, but some of the groundwork for empathy can be done through simpler techniques such as persona development. Personas are essentially mock representations of different types of customers. The attributes used to define the personas can vary tremendously based on the purpose, focusing on income, gender, geography, purchasing habits, driving patterns, and so on. We often recommend adding "information appetite" and "channel preference" to the list of attributes considered in personas. These address how much and in what medium people prefer to interact. For a Wall Street brokerage, knowing whether a customer prefers to trade directly online or through a broker might be a critical differentiator in determining how to simplify the customer experience.

With social media, the opportunities to listen to people— and to actually hear what they're saying as they discuss aspirations, needs, and dreams—have never been more plentiful. A point to bear in mind about new media: There's a world of difference between using it to connect with consumers and using it to track them online (we tend to think of "cookies" as a cute euphemism for "bloody footprints"). There is nothing empathetic about encroaching on people's privacy. In fact, it's another way the company can end up distancing itself from the very consumers it wants to get to know better.

One of the keys to presenting clear and simple information is to understand your audience—and respect the diversity of that audience. Yet it's amazing how many programs and documents created by well-meaning government agencies can be culturally tone-deaf. For example, a free school lunch application has a very specific audience (people who have low incomes and children in school). So a question such as the following might seem quite innocuous and straightforward to a middle-class, educated, American-born graphic designer, while being frightening and off-putting to a recent immigrant:

> If any child you are applying for is homeless, migrant, or a runaway, please call this number: Ann Smith, 555-5555 ext. 555.
> - ☐ Homeless
> - ☐ Migrant
> - ☐ Runaway

It's easy to envision someone believing that if they answer this, the authorities will come knocking—not to help, but to remove the child.

No matter how worthy the cause, outreach attempts can fall flat if they fail to recognize or respect cultural biases and attitudes of the intended audience. For example, attempts to increase the use of automobile child restraints in minority neighborhoods have tended to have a low success rate in the past, but a notable exception was a program conducted in a Hispanic neighborhood in Dallas, which after a short time produced dramatic results. What made it work? The program administrators immersed themselves in the local culture. They figured out the best venues to spread the message and found ways to incorporate religion and cultural beliefs into the program. (For example, at the local church, priests were asked to bless the child safety seats in a ceremony before they were distributed.) Understanding what would motivate parents meant researching their values, not just their literacy skills.[10]

Ideally, everything a company puts out there—from its products and services to its website to every letter or invoice sent to customers—should reflect its commitment to considering the customer's point of view. We're all looking for that in our interactions with organizations and companies—the sense that someone there is aware of us as human beings. This can be expressed in the most minor exchanges and in mundane forms of communication. From clear instruction manuals to statements and invoices that are easy to read and understand, there are many ways to signal to customers that you're a company that understands and respects them.

It always amazes us when companies spend millions burnishing their brands and then undermine it with the stroke of a pen. The truth is, every bit of correspondence you send to customers—email correspondence, statements, contracts, proposals, instructions, applications, call center scripts—speaks louder than your ads, because it's a more direct and personal form of contact. Each of these **unheralded touchpoints** should be treated as a hot button—a make-or-break moment in the customer relationship (see Figure 3.1). Each one should convey the sense that it's been customized for the individual consumer, and each one should be infused with the attributes and qualities that define the brand.

There is an interesting circular effect at work here. Because sales contracts, insurance policies, legal agreements, and product instructions are so frequently confusing and off-putting, people naturally tend to dislike or ignore them. Companies react to this by deciding they don't want to spend the time and money to make things clear; as they see it, "the customers just don't care about this stuff." This creates a dismissive corporate attitude surrounding routine communications—that they're just "necessary evils" or "paperwork." Then organizations delegate the creation of documents and websites to the techies or lawyers, who modify rather than innovate. More often than not, the communication ends up being wordy, disorganized, imprecise, and redundant. And the cycle continues—a major

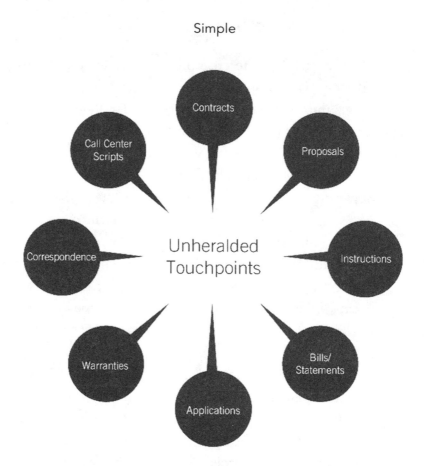

Figure 3.1

problem for business, because unheralded touchpoints form the core of day-to-day relationships with customers. These interactions are lost opportunities to build trust between companies and customers and reduce customer defection.

Rather than a company claiming it is "easy to do business with," it is more effective to let them experience it for themselves. Pay attention to each interaction, no matter how small.

Companies that do a better job of simplifying their communications spend far less time—and money—talking on the phone to confused (and possibly angry) customers. Future sales can also be affected: Our own "Perplexity Polls" show that as a result of unclear product instructions, consumers were not only more likely to contact the manufacturer or seller of a product; they were also less inclined to purchase another product from that company.

Sometimes, even in spite of your best efforts to provide simple and clear communication in all other forms, people are still going to call your company. When that happens, here's a tip: Answer the phone. Especially if you're a phone company. Not long ago, we had a telephone company client that wanted to take the customer service phone number off the bill because having it there might "encourage people to call." When the phone company doesn't want us to make phone calls, you know something's gone wrong.

> Often the simplest interaction is for a customer to speak to a person within a company. Yet companies have made that a privilege. As the marketing blogger B. L. Ochman recently pointed out, only three of the Fortune 50 companies include a phone number on their website home page—and some don't even have a contact link.[11]

This is one of the ways companies end up distancing themselves from customers—by in effect putting up a wall. That wall may take the form of an automated phone tree, an outsourced call center, or other attempts to avoid direct human contact. The funny thing is, a lot of these automated tools were *supposed* to simplify business—and yet they can end up having the opposite effect on your customers. Technology can do amazing things, but when a human being has a particular question or a problem, the simplest and most satisfying way to resolve it is usually person to person.

It is possible to streamline operations without sacrificing the human element of customer service. ING Direct has a lean and mean operation, but it still encourages customers to call with questions or problems. Southwest Airlines specializes in trimming the fat from its operations, but it has always put a premium on improving human contact with passengers.

Some of this flies in the face of the prevalent view that business must cut costs to the bone, especially in lean times. Simplification can indeed be an excellent way to lower costs, but not if it involves scaling back on customer service. When companies try to save money on outsourced customer service, phone trees, or form-letter responses, they destroy any chance of developing meaningful relationships with consumers.

And by the way, if you do a decent job answering those phones, it may actually boost profits. According to a recent study by the UK firm Harding & Yorke, there was a strong link between companies that placed more emphasis on the quality and empathy level of call responses (which included encouraging call center agents to spend more time trying to relate to callers and better understand their issues) and the profitability of those companies.[12]

In the business world, the notion that it might be important to "put oneself in the place of others" has only lately begun to gain credence. For corporate executives who've been trained to think of customers as "targets," it can be a leap to make the decision to embrace empathy—not as a "soft" emotion, but as a business practice. Yet this is a critical first step toward achieving simplicity. It makes it possible to move on to some other vital steps.

CHAPTER 4
....

Distill

ONCE YOU HAVE A BETTER UNDERSTANDING OF
NEEDS, YOU CAN MAKE INFORMED DECISIONS
ON BEHALF OF OTHERS. TO SIMPLIFY IS TO
CURATE, EDIT—AND LESSEN THE OPTIONS AND
CHOICES THAT OVERWHELM.

When Google introduced its now famous search engine, it wasn't the first to offer search capability to consumers. But Google's version quickly left competitors behind, gaining mainstream acceptance. And as many observers have noted in the years since, the simplicity of Google's home page had much to do with its appeal and success. In fact, when we recently surveyed more than six thousand respondents worldwide for the Siegel+Gale 2011 Global Brand Simplicity Index, one brand stood above all the rest: Google. People rate it the highest of any brand out there in terms of delivering a clean, simple, rewarding experience.[1]

But why was Google the only one to make its search page so simple and uncluttered? Shouldn't other search firms have done likewise with their offerings? If, in this case, less is clearly more, then why not just offer less? It would seem to be not only the smartest but also the easiest option for a company producing a search page.

> *"Focusing is about saying no. You've got to say no, no, no. The result of that focus is going to be some really great products where the total is much greater than the sum of the parts."[2]*
> —STEVE JOBS

But in fact it can be much harder to simplify—which may explain why Google was the only one to offer such a clean page. So how did Google resist the temptation to add on and complicate? We talked to the Mountain View, California–based company about this, and learned a couple of surprising things.

Google didn't just stumble into its home page design; it didn't arrive at simplicity by default. The company actually developed a rigorous system that imposed tight restrictions upon what could and could not be added to the page. Its leaders had to stand firm against Google's own creative and well-meaning engineers. And in some cases they even had to defy the wishes of customers.

This ongoing task of holding the line against complexity—which often involves being willing to "just say no" to additional features, design flourishes, and other potential complications—often fell to Marissa Mayer, until recently the company's director of consumer web products. When we spoke to Mayer about how she managed this, she surprised us by using a word you tend to hear from theatrical casting directors, not tech managers. Mayer explained that any potential new feature hoping to get on the Google home page must go through an "audition." First the feature is tried out on Google's advanced search page to see how it performs there. But even if the new idea demonstrates its viability in the advanced search, it still goes through a tough scoring system developed by Google.

Here's how the scoring system works:

1. They assign a point for each change in type style, type size, or color.
2. They add the points; the maximum allowed for a promotion is three points.

The goal for the home page is the fewest possible number of points. As Mayer says, "More points equals less simplicity."

This stripped-down approach could easily lead to a home page that would be pristine but devoid of humanity. Google's page is anything but that. Millions of people log on to the Google home page just to see the ever-changing dressing of its logo. Google understood that while many elements on the home page could be considered extraneous, it was important to have something—even just one small, playful touch—that would convey the brand personality. In many ways, Google is a utility like toothpaste, but as Mayer says, "Imagine if your toothpaste tube had unpredictable, whimsical designs on it." That would change your perception of the toothpaste maker. The company is so focused on simplicity that it refuses to be led astray—even by its own customers. For example, when Google surveys users to see if they wanted more search results per page, they invariably say yes—who wouldn't want more results to choose from? But, Mayer says, "We don't give it to them." Google knows that offering more results will take longer to load, which will slow down and ultimately diminish the user's experience—even if most people don't realize this. "Customers often don't understand the consequences of their choices, but it is our job to do so," Mayer says. "We figured out that ten results per page is the right number. We don't change that." In other words, Google has the guts to give customers less, even when they ask for more.

Simplification is often about narrowing the scope of what you offer as you try to serve those needs. Successful simplifiers distill whatever they're offering down to its essence. It's one of the most challenging aspects of simplification, because distillation requires focus and discipline in the face of the constant temptation to add on, expand, and complicate.

Anyone trying to create a simple *anything*—a product, a piece of communication, a service, an experience, a law or regulation—

> "Simplicity is an exact medium between too little and too much."
> —Joshua Reynolds, eighteenth-century English painter

must be ruthless when it comes to editing, purifying, or, to use a harsher word, *killing*. Hollywood filmmakers often use the term "killing your babies" when referring to a scriptwriter's painful task of deleting something he loves—a colorful scene, a quirky character, an oh-so-clever line—that just doesn't advance the story. If filmmakers didn't kill their babies regularly, they'd be producing four-hour films with diluted messages that would make viewers want their four hours and fifteen bucks back. Similarly, when simplifying products, services, communications, or even entire business models, there's no substitute for being a ruthless killer.

The challenge is knowing what to kill and what to keep—what's essential and what isn't. Companies can and should rely on consumers to help them figure that out through research, though it's important to note that the customer isn't always right about this, as Google has shown. People have a tendency to want "more" even if it's not necessarily good for them. And marketers have a tendency to offer them "more" in order to make the easy sale.

To some extent, the quest for simplicity in the consumer marketplace comes down to short-term impulses versus long-term interests. John Maeda, president of the Rhode Island School of Design and a longtime student of simplicity, points out that most people are wired to want more. "More is safety," he says. When a consumer is making purchasing choices, the product with more features may seem appealing—but that appeal doesn't necessarily endure after the purchase has been made. "At the point of desire you want more," Maeda has observed, "but at the point of daily use, you want less."[3]

So what happens when that feature-laden product is brought home? Too often, people have no idea what to do with it. A recent study found that half the gadgets returned are actually in good working order, but customers can't figure out how to operate them. The study found that on average, Americans are willing to spend about twenty minutes trying to figure out how to work a new toy, at which point they tend to give up and bring it back to the store.[4] The cost of returned products in the United States is $100 billion a year.

And that's not counting what it costs companies in terms of reputation and customer loyalty. Many consumers, having been burned once by an overly complex product, are reluctant to buy that brand again. They may become reluctant to buy any kind of high-tech gadget: Research from the Yankee Group found that 50 percent of people postpone electronics purchases, thinking that the product will be too difficult to use.

This creates a conundrum for product engineers and marketers. The usability expert Jasper van Kuijk, a researcher at TU Delft (Delft University of Technology, in the Netherlands) who has worked closely with Philips and other companies, observes that when companies make things simple and usable for customers, people are more likely to use and enjoy the product—contributing to customer satisfaction and a brand's long-term success. However, "If a company is looking for a short-term win or immediate sale, then simplicity doesn't necessarily give you that because it's often not a purchase consideration," van Kuijk says. "In fact what is most commercially attractive may be more features and functionality—so it can be a risky sales strategy to limit a product to the most basic features."[5]

And the pressure to offer "more" isn't just coming from consumers. From a marketing standpoint, companies try to one-up competitors. They also strive to appeal to as many potential consumers as possible—after all, who knows which add-on feature may be the one that closes the sale? So the video camera gets more and more buttons, offering more ways to frame, zoom, and edit, as the instruction manual grows thicker. And the whole thing ends up sitting unused in the closet.

Every once in a while, someone figures out that none of this makes sense. A few years ago, when the small start-up tech company Pure Digital and its design partner, Smart Design, introduced the Flip Video camcorder, this minimalist product—it had no buttons other than one big red one, which was all you needed to push to start and stop filming—was hailed by the *Wall Street Journal* as "stunningly simple."[6] Usability expert van Kuijk observed, "The Flip was amazing when it came out because at the time, everyone was making these very elaborate products, with more zoom and pixels. And the Flip had no special settings, basically anyone could use it—even kids in kindergarten could use it to make videos."

That level of sheer simplicity was no accident, of course.

Throughout the entire process of developing the Flip, according to Smart Design's Nasahn Sheppard, "We were constantly asking 'What can we take out?' not 'What can we put in?'"

Indeed, the product development process on the Flip began and ended with one driving thought: Keep it simple. This insight was forged by empathy. Through extensive observation, researchers at Smart Design and Pure Digital became aware that there was one very large problem with camcorders that the industry didn't seem to want to acknowledge—you might say it was the elephant in the room (or, more accurately, on the top shelf of the closet). People were simply not using their video cameras because their owners found them to be overly complicated, bulky, intrusive, and incapable of "capturing the moment." People needed something they could spontaneously pull out of their pocket and start using immediately, wherever they happened to be. As van Kuijk points out, video camera makers, who'd gotten caught up in their features arms race, forgot the basic point that "the best camera is the one you take with you and actually use."

This realization drove the entire product development process, says Smart Design's Richard Whitehall. Whenever somebody thought about adding another feature or button, they were reminded of the main rationale behind this product—ease of use. "You have to clearly define that core purpose of whatever you're designing early in the process, and get everyone to agree on it," says Whitehall. It's the only way to avoid "feature creep," which occurs naturally because "even though you may start out trying to solve one main problem," Whitehall says, "along the way you're bound to realize, 'Well, we could also solve this other problem, and maybe that one, too—and it could possibly expand our base of customers.' So you always have to ask, 'At what cost?'"

The engineers and designers at both Pure Digital and Smart had to keep reminding their bosses—and themselves—that the main problem they needed to solve was that people too often "missed the moment" with their video cameras, so the Flip's makers had one inviolable law: The product had to remain so uncluttered and easy to use that within thirty seconds of first seeing a Flip, anyone would know how to operate it.

It isn't easy to create a simple product. It involves constant trade-offs (what do we keep/what do we kill?), as well as the need to find the right balance between quality, functionality (how much should the product be able to do?), and ease of use. Added to this mix is cosmetic design, which is also important: A simple product should look the part. Much of Apple's success can be attributed to its ability to hit a "grand slam" on its best products—combining quality, multifunctionality, ease of use, and simple, elegant appearance.

"[Good design] captures customers' trust by disappearing."[7]
—JACK DORSEY, COFOUNDER OF TWITTER

Flip's designers wanted the product not only to appear simple but also to be easy to use and deliver high-quality results, so they went easy on multifunctionality. The camera only had to do a couple of things: take great videos and make them easy to share on YouTube. To allow for the latter, the design included a flip-open USB connection so you could plug right into your computer after shooting something—no need for memory cards, cables, software, discs, and so forth.

In lieu of bells and whistles, the Flip makers focused on video quality. The finished product was pocket-sized, though it could have been even smaller and thinner; Pure Digital opted to use a high-quality lens. The product had to be *good*, as well as simple. To that end, they also developed built-in exposure control algorithms to make sure the picture maintained a smooth look over a range of lighting conditions. That required some complex engineering—but you'd never know it to look at the finished product. All of that exposure control was happening *inside* the product, out of view and without requiring the user to do anything. In this regard, the designers were following one of the most basic—and important—rules of "simple design": Whenever possible, complexity should be moved out of the user's way and out of sight.

The Flip sold two million units in its first six months, becoming the top-selling camcorder on the market. It had an impressive 37 percent market share as of 2011, when something unexpected happened: Cisco Systems, after acquiring Pure Digital, announced that it was discontinuing the product. How could such a beautifully simple creation (and such a strong performer in the marketplace) meet such a fate?

One theory is that the world's simplest video camera was done in by the master simplifier himself, Steve Jobs—who by early 2011 had figured out how to incorporate high-quality video into the newest version of the iPhone. This may have convinced Cisco that the Flip's days were numbered, because after all, who would need a separate video camera if you had one built into your smartphone? The answer to that actually depends on whether one thinks there is still a place in the world for products that do one thing simply and well. The iPhone does many things, some better than others, and while it's not hard to use the iPhone's video camera, it's definitely not as simple as pushing that one red button on the dear departed Flip.

Smart Design's Nasahn Sheppard maintains that the Flip would've done just fine going head to head with the iPhone. There are times when people want a phone to be just a phone, and a video camera to be just a video camera. Sheppard points to Amazon's Kindle reader: "The Kindle has the potential to do more, but Amazon has shown restraint to keep it simple and focused on the pleasures of long-form reading." He added, "In some contexts, it's just better to do one thing really well instead of five things adequately."

That's the thinking behind the recent emergence of super-simple cell phones such as the Jitterbug and John's Phone. Hein Mevissen and Diederiekje Bok, the Dutch cocreators of John's Phone, found themselves looking at all the overloaded cell phones on the market and asking: Why can't a phone just make phone calls? Why does it have to do *everything*?

And so amid a sea of Motorola Droid X2s, HTC Evo Shift

4Gs, Samsung Galaxy S IIs, and RIM BlackBerry Curves, they envisioned a supremely simple phone with a plain name. John's Phone has an interface that consists of just an oversized number pad and graphic call and hang-up keys. Its purpose is to make calls, of course, but you might say its higher purpose is to avoid the frustrating complications that come with smartphone use—hard to dial, battery's gone dead, can't get a signal, and so on. This phone's battery can be used for a month without recharging, and it has the ability to make and receive calls anywhere around the globe. The phone has been catching on with people trying to make an anti-tech statement, and it seems tailor-made for elementary schoolers, people with aging eyes or big thumbs, and, of course, people named John. It's styled as "no-nonsense" (or what some just call "sense")—you call, you talk, you hang up.[8]

Interestingly, one of the people trying to simplify cell phones today is married to the man who invented them in the first place. Arlene Harris's husband, Martin Cooper, developed the first cellular phone for Motorola back in the 1970s. That original creation was designed to just make calls while on the go (which seems kind of quaint now, doesn't it?). As the cell phone subsequently added so many features that it was eventually deemed "smart," Arlene saw a need to go back to basics. So she created the Jitterbug phone, in partnership with Samsung

Electronics. It shares some of the simple qualities of John's Phone but goes a step further in terms of catering to the needs of older people.[9]

The phone has features that make it comfortable and easy for seniors—or anyone, for that matter—to use. One example is a padded earpiece that cups the ear to reduce outside noise; another is a volume adjustment that increases sound clarity. But what's more interesting are some of the things the phone lacks. It is completely devoid of icons, as well as decision trees and buttons that have to be held for several seconds to turn the phone on or off. Rather, the phone has a physical on/off button devoted to those functions alone. Jitterbug doesn't require passwords because some older people find them hard to remember. (Come to think of it, don't we all?)

And gone is the tedium of reading an instruction manual and spending hours programming the phone after purchase. Jitterbug is only purchasable by phone or online through a highly personalized experience—a human customer service representative at Jitterbug's parent company, Great Call, customizes the phone to include features the person will actually use and even enters their frequently called phone numbers before the phone is shipped.

One of the design mandates was that actions should be "familiar"—so they used an innovative "recipe card" format for the instructions that fits in a folder. Only one feature is described per card. That way, the phone can be shipped with only the pages relevant to the features that were chosen by the buyer. Similarly, they are working on a one-fold, postcard-size bill.

To customize the phone to the differing needs of the fifty-five-plus market, there are actually two versions of the Jitterbug phone. One has a regular keypad (with good-sized, easy-to-dial buttons), while the other, referred to as "One Touch Jitterbug," has just three keys—for 911, the Great Call Operator, and a custom button. This version is intended for seniors who don't think that they need a cell phone, but their children do.

We like almost everything about the Jitterbug (including the name, chosen because, as Harris told us, "that word, and picturing the dance step, just makes you smile"), but what really impresses is the empathy shown for seniors. Jitterbug understands and anticipates their needs—the product solves old problems for them instead of creating new ones. It's logical that some of the best simplification efforts right now are coming from innovators trying to serve the needs of seniors and aging boomers. When you design for older consumers, you have no choice but to simplify—there's a built-in discipline that encourages the makers of these products and services to distill, focus, clarify. But as the crisis of complexity engulfs more and more of us, regardless of age, we're going to face the same problems that John's Phone and Jitterbug are trying to solve.

This notion that sometimes it's better to have fewer options, as opposed to an endless array of possibilities to choose from, shouldn't be a radical idea—yet somehow in the current culture it is. Both consumers and companies have come to believe that in a free marketplace, within a free society, choice is always a good thing. But in fusing the noble goal of self-determination with the difficult realities of decision making, we end up with a situation where people are overwhelmed and feel inadequate if they admit confusion.

> The typical Safeway supermarket stocks forty thousand SKUs. With just one-tenth that number of items, the store could cover 95 percent of customer needs, says consultant Peter Sealey of the Sausalito Group.

Providing endless choice is also a convenient way of passing the buck. It allows businesses (and sometimes government) to say, "We don't want to do the hard job of figuring out what people actually want or need, and then winnowing down the choices that best fit those wants/needs. So instead we'll offer everything—what more could they want?"

Peter Sealey, CEO and founder of the Sausalito Group, Inc., a highly regarded management consulting firm, has been advocating simplification for decades, ever since his days as an executive at Coca-Cola, where he experienced firsthand a kind of arms race among competing brand managers. "At one point, there were sixty-seven or sixty-eight SKUs for one brand of Coca-Cola," Sealey says. "It happened because brand managers said, 'If we add another flavor or one more size, we'll sell more units this year.' But incrementally doing this year after year, there is absolute clutter."[10]

The dirty secret is that trying to give people everything is a lousy business model. It overwhelms customers, at which point they may just default to "no" since they can't make up their minds. It clutters stores and undermines the shopping experience. And on top of all that it's inefficient in terms of managing all that inventory. The supermarket chain Trader Joe's figured this out and decided to distill the supermarket shopping experience down to something much more manageable.

The chain, which has about 350 stores in the United States, recently was dubbed "one of the hottest retailers in the U.S." by *Fortune* magazine, "elevating food shopping from a chore to a cultural experience."[11] And one of the key ways Trader Joe's does this is by offering *much less* than other supermarkets (about four thousand SKUs instead of forty thousand).

For this approach to work, Trader Joe's has to make smart choices on behalf of its customers. The company does extensive research on its customer base and knows what they tend to like and not like. They want good prices; they like a bit of fun and adventurous flavor (Trader Joe's responds by mixing in some exotic food choices and using playful, quirky packaging); and they trust that the Trader Joe's house brand will live up to expectations.

By having less clutter, Trader Joe's creates a neighborhood

market aura in its stores. But it also makes sense from a financial standpoint. The stores have very high sales revenues per square foot, in part because if you're offering fewer brands, you sell more items per brand, which in turn means you get better pricing discounts from suppliers. As *Fortune* noted, "It makes the whole business—from stocking shelves to checking out customers—much simpler."

Increasingly, we're seeing all kinds of retailers beginning to embrace the less-is-more strategy, from the big-box chains, who've recently been experimenting with small-store formats, to specialty stores narrowing their focus in terms of the merchandise they carry. At the extreme you have a retailer in Japan that each day offers only three—count 'em, *three*—products, as a way of focusing consumer attention on those products.[12] With this approach, the retailer acts as curator, as in, *We've sifted through everything, and this is what we think you're going to find most interesting.*

It's not just cluttered stores that need good curators to simplify the experience; the World Wide Web requires this kind of distillation even more. Ray Weaver, a professor at the Harvard Business School, has observed that some of today's most successful web businesses—Facebook in particular—have taken on a role very similar to that of a museum curator. When we visit a large museum, Weaver points out, "We appreciate that [there is] an expert who functions as our decision-making proxy," because we know that this helps make the museum-going experience more manageable and meaningful. We don't have time to see everything, so curators edit out the less important works; they make choices about which pieces should go together—and explain why we should care.[13]

In much the same way, Facebook's success is based on its ability to "curate" the otherwise overwhelming experience of dealing with the World Wide Web. Weaver cites "the control Facebook exerts over the environment"—taking web search, content, email, and bringing it into a structured environment, "an orderly alternative to the Web."

However, the curator model can break down when the curator fails to do a good job of editing, distilling, and choosing. Some of Facebook's redesign fiascos suggest that although the company may have started out as a simplifier, it has lately fallen prey to the temptation to overload its eight hundred million customers.

When Facebook redesigned its site in the fall of 2011, a poll by the website *Mashable* found that 75 percent of Facebook fans "hated" the redesign.[14] One particularly vociferous critic, Chris Taylor, listed some of the ways Facebook had turned a simple design into an overly complex one. The site's new "Ticker" real-time stream of information "now crowds the right-side of your Facebook page with a lot of distracting noise," Taylor wrote on *Mashable*. Meanwhile, Facebook "couldn't leave well enough alone" with its popular "Like" feature and added "Facebook Gestures," which open up the door for using all sorts of verbs beyond "Like." And instead of just "friending" people, with the new design you had to decide if you want to subscribe to their feeds.[15]

Worst of all, in the eyes of Taylor and other critics, was the new feature called Timeline, telling your whole life story in chronological order. (Even among the compulsive info-sharers on Facebook, this struck many as a case of "too much information.") The *New York Times* columnist David Pogue was not quite as unforgiving as Taylor, but still complained about "the increasing number of roadblocks Facebook's new design throws in the path of doing something that should be easy."[16]

Why would Facebook mess with a perfectly good, simple design? Because it just can't resist, Taylor theorized. The company is top-heavy with engineers who want to show off new features they've developed. Its marketers, meanwhile, are looking for new ways to extract customer information that might be appealing to advertisers.

The decisions made in distilling and editing shouldn't be based on what the competition is doing or on the wish lists of the company's engineers and marketers. Every choice should be based on trying to produce the most rewarding customer experience.

Figuring out how to do that is never easy—but there are more tools and means for tackling the challenge than ever before. Apps are already having a positive effect. Mobile apps, delivered on small screens, impose size restrictions that have forced developers to distill their messages. It's interesting to compare websites and apps from the same company—such as the Bloomberg example shown. What you often find is that apps (see Figure 4.1) are focused, uncluttered, and useful, while the websites remain jumbled, muddied, and distracting. Websites typically have too much going on visually and look like a "land grab" on the part of all the departments in a company vying for space. The appeal of apps is their specificity—usually one or a few purposes—and their visual appeal, which is eye-catching, uncluttered, and inviting. As companies catch on to this, they will apply the power of brevity and clarity to other communications.

New technology is also now making it possible to distill,

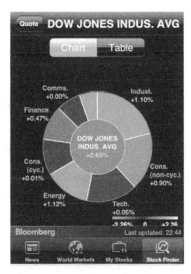

Figure 4.1   The mobile app is clear and focused.

filter, and customize offerings based on individual customer preferences. That's what Pandora's customized Internet radio service is all about.[17]

If we think of simplification as a shortening of the distance between sender (seller) and receiver (buyer), there are a number of ways to achieve this. The seller can communicate so clearly and present options so simply that you easily recognize what you want to buy. But another approach, made possible by technology, is to create a "decision filter" to deliver the perfect choice without my having to make a laborious decision.

Pandora's cofounder, Tim Westergren, had both a technology and a music business background, and his goal was to use computer algorithms to match particular songs and musicians with listeners' personal tastes. The company creates a collection of customized radio stations for each individual listener with music you might enjoy.

Westergren's challenge was to distill music down to its essence. His "Music Genome Project," which had its structural underpinnings in biology and in the notion that if you could codify the basic elements of music—the beats, the tones, the chords—you could then determine which combinations appeal to particular people's tastes and predict what music they'd like.

Westergren described this system as "a hand-built musical taxonomy that captures an immense amount of musicological details across hundreds of thousands of songs." All that hand-building was done by the company's musicologists, who studied songs and broke them down into hundreds of distinguishing characteristics per song. (Is it upbeat? Does it feature certain types of instruments? Is the lead singer's voice raspy?)

If this sounds like a complex task, it was—but the result for listeners was wonderfully simple. Once Pandora had developed its system for mapping the DNA of music, all you had to do was input basic information telling Pandora that your favorite song was, for example, "Mood Indigo," and it could create a Mood Indigo station for you, offering up a steady stream of songs that shared some of the same musical "genes." The more input you give Pandora, the better it tends to get at customizing music for your tastes.

Pandora's approach runs counter to the idea that music lovers want to be offered infinite choice from massive online catalogs. Indeed, some other Internet music services have much larger libraries than Pandora, giving listeners access to millions of songs. But Westergren is not concerned with the biggest catalogs, with the most songs. "This may seem counter-intuitive," he told the *New York Times Magazine*, "but we struggle more with making sure we're adding really good stuff."

With more than forty million listeners, Pandora is now testing to see if its "smart filtering" approach can be extended beyond music, into areas such as comedy. (Pandora recently introduced customized comedy stations as part of its Internet radio offering.) After all, if you can map the DNA of a song, why not a joke? Indeed, why not a lot of things? It seems logical that this genomic approach could be applied to customizing lots of services, thereby simplifying consumer decisions in any number of areas.

Letting customers decide how much info they want

Almost any business category could benefit from finding ways to distill and filter massive amounts of information. A prime candidate is financial services. The average investor is faced with thousands of options and endless possibilities, resulting in decision paralysis. As we've worked with various Wall Street brokerage firms over the years to redesign their customer account statements, we've always stressed that filtering of information was needed—and that customers' appetite for information does not correlate to the amount of money they have. Some people are naturally bookkeeping types who want detail. Others only want summary information. These personality traits do not seem to be linked to how much money a person has. Up until we worked with Edward Jones, a brokerage firm headquartered in St. Louis, our clients always insisted on sending more detail to wealthier clients, against our advice.

With the largest number of branches of any investment firm in the United States, Edward Jones treats its customers as individuals rather than as accounts. The firm seized upon the idea of letting customers choose the amount of detail they wanted in their statements. They could choose from three types of statements with differing levels of information:

- At-a-glance
- Preferred
- In-depth

The "At-a-glance" statement format is only one page and includes less account data but more definitions, annotations, and helpful explanations. It appeals to investors with little experience or knowledge of financial markets.

The "Preferred" statement format appeals to investors who have a basic understanding of the markets but look to the experts for advice and direction. This format has additional content such as gain/loss information and is the default for customers who do not specify which level of detail they want.

The "In-depth" statement format includes content of interest to more analytical investors, bond maturity schedules and asset allocation graph comparisons of target versus current distribution of assets in the account. The investors who have chosen this format have a keen interest and sophisticated understanding of their assets, transactions, and investing potential.

So what did people choose? Interestingly, 90 percent fall into the "Preferred" segment, with just 5 percent apiece in each of the other two. When we interviewed Daniel Burkhardt, a partner at Edward Jones and manager of the project, we found his take on this skew insightful. "The Preferred ended up so readable that it cannibalized the market for the At-a-glance format. Investors felt comfortable that they understood the mid-level detail."

This suggests that financial customers at all levels are looking for distillation of information, but not necessarily to the point of losing access to critical data. The beauty of what Edward Jones did here was to create different levels of filtering—and then allow customers to figure out which level is right for them.

*   *   *

The bottom line: Don't assume that by giving your customers "more" (whether it's more information, options, features, mustards, or songs), you're doing them any favors. When you distill an offering down to its essence—even though it may seem on the surface that you're asking people to settle for less choice—you're more apt to provide a purer, simpler, more satisfying experience.

Many people mistakenly believe there is a conflict between innovation and simplicity, that in order to move forward you must somehow add to what already exists. But sometimes what you take away can be just as important.

CHAPTER 5

Clarify

"TOO MUCH INFORMATION" IS A PRIME SOURCE
OF COMPLEXITY.

What inspires someone to simplify? In Deborah Adler's case, it was a personal mission. Confusing prescription labels had threatened the health of a family member, and Adler was determined to do something about it.[1]

It began when Adler's grandmother suddenly fell ill—sick to her stomach—for no apparent reason. Eventually, a doctor determined the source of the problem: The older woman had accidentally taken her husband's prescription medicine instead of her own. After treatment, she quickly recovered.

But Adler, a grad student at the time, was left wondering: How does a mix-up like this happen? Then she took a peek into her grandparents' medicine cabinet and found the answer. She saw rows of identical small brown prescription drug vials, each one bearing a medicine label that was practically unreadable even to the young Adler.

Adler did some research and learned a couple of interesting things. There's an ongoing epidemic of people mistakenly taking the wrong medications—more than half of Americans have done so at one time or another. But in spite of this, no one had thought to do anything about those hard-to-read labels on prescription bottles that had been used for decades. Adler created her own test version of a different kind of prescription drug bottle and label to address the problem.

First, she focused on all the small type on the typical drug label. Adler happened to have a design education background, but as she told us, "Anyone with common sense could tell there was too much information on the labels and it wasn't organized or presented with any kind of thought." With one exception, that is: On most labels, the large colorful logo for the pharmacy (arguably the least important bit of information) was the only thing that stood out.

Adler sought to arrange the information in a logical order, giving prominence to the things people most need to know at the moment they're reaching for their medicine. Having read up on cognitive schemas—a psychological term that refers to the ways people take in and organize information—she knew it was important to try to anticipate what people might want to know first, second, and third. So she decided the label should zero in on these three important facts:

1. Who the medicine is for;
2. The name of the drug and dosage;
3. How to take it.

Adler divided the drug label into two parts separated by a thick black line in the middle. The critical information went into the top section, while everything else was relegated to the bottom.

Next Adler decided to rethink the shape of the bottles. On conventional rounded vials it can be hard to read the wrap-around labels; you have to turn the bottle as you read. Adler thought, why can't a medicine bottle be flat? She ended up using a flat tube that stood upright on its cap, with plenty of room for a large flat label that could be read in one glance.

Thinking of the mix-up involving her grandparents, Adler felt it was important to distinguish between medicine bottles of different family members who might be sharing the same cabinet. She thought about how she and her husband kept their toothbrushes separate by using different colors. "So I figured, why can't medicine bottles also be color-coded?" Adler created color rings for each family member.

The last change involved the warnings on drug labels— often a source of confusion. Working with the designer Milton Glaser, she replaced old instructions with new, more intuitive icons. (For example, a warning to pregnant women featured a silhouette of a pregnant woman's body.)

Adler's endeavor to create simpler, clearer drug packaging served as the basis of her master's thesis, but soon became something more. After she presented a sample of her redesign to representatives of the Target retail chain, Target bought the idea and rushed a new line of prescription drug bottles to market in 2005. Adler's "ClearRx" prescription system has been used by Target pharmacies ever since.

Adler herself was transformed along with those drug bottles. She now runs a small design firm dedicated primarily to simplifying and bringing greater clarity to various medical products and services—everything from packaging of hospital bandages to catheter systems. "There's too much complexity in healthcare today," she told us. "Sometimes, treatment has to be complex. But prevention is often a matter of simplifying things so that people understand what they should and shouldn't be doing." How does she create that simplicity? "I think simplicity is rooted in empathy and insight. In my case, it's about paying attention as I walk around a hospital to try to see where the problems are and what could be improved. It can be about putting yourself in someone else's shoes, then going through the steps they go through—such as when they open a medicine cabinet and reach for their pills. What's getting in their way? How can we improve that situation?"

Deborah Adler's story shows what can happen when complexity invades our lives, finding its way into our homes and even our medicine cabinets. This is far from an isolated incident: What happened to Adler's grandmother is happening so often, to so many, that according to the health research organization NEIH, people's inability to follow drug instructions results in $290 billion in medical expenses each year.[2]

Consider some of the sources of confusion currently adding to this crisis:

- **People can't make heads or tails of warning label icons.** As the *New York Times* recently pointed out, drug warning labels are not standardized, regulated, or even reviewed by the FDA, and worse than that, they're using fine print that can't be read and icons that are downright confusing. On one label, an icon of the sun with a slash through it was supposed to warn people to avoid prolonged exposure to sunlight while taking the medicine—but many thought it meant "Don't leave this medicine in the sun!"[3]

- **They can't keep up with ever-expanding lists of side effects.** Drug labels, on average, now list seventy possible side effects (some list as many as five hundred). By treating even the most infrequent or minor side effects the same as more serious ones, the lists overwhelm people—and end up being ignored.[4]

- **They can't (or won't) wade through pages of instruction from the pharmacist.** Consumers now get up to three different types of drug pamphlets (from the manufacturer, the FDA, and the drugstore) with prescriptions—providing too much information, some of it conflicting. Single-page information sheets are needed to replace the multipage package inserts and guides used with many drugs.

These are sobering facts for the pharmaceutical industry. But the problem of unclear instructions extends well beyond drug labels and touches on many areas of business, government, and daily life. Far too many companies and government agencies are having trouble communicating the basic information people need to use products and services.

Want to install a car seat? Should be fairly easy, right? Not according to a recent study showing that 80 percent of child safety seats are improperly installed or misused and the instructions for installing them are the root of the problem.[5] For one thing, those instructions are written at a tenth-grade reading level, while at least 50 percent of U.S. adults read at a significantly lower level.

How about parking your car? How hard could that be? Well, if you're in New York City, you must somehow decipher the street sign shown in Figure 5.1. The sign is laughable, but the hundreds of dollars in fines (and towing of your car) aren't. Certainly techno-

Figure 5.1

logy should be able to correct this by allowing you to use a smartphone to scan a sign and get a message customized by date and time to tell you whether you can park worry-free at that moment.

It gets worse, however: Unclear instructions not only can empty your wallet; they can actually kill you. In September 2006, a Legacy 600 private jet crashed into a Boeing 737 in South America, killing 154 people. As a fascinating report in *Vanity Fair* revealed, the two pilots of the smaller plane were flying a new but "inherently simple jet that had been stuffed with electronic capabilities—most of them nested, and therefore hidden from immediate view." The pilots were unable to answer a simple question ("how much longer to the destination?") because the computer screen offered them:

Duty Time, Block Time, Local Time, Push Time, Release Time, Time Off, Time en Route, Time of Arrival, Fuel-Remaining Time, Void Time, Expect-This-or-That Time. There is also Coordinated Universal Time, called Zulu Time.

At some point during their fumbling and searching for information they needed, the pilots turned off the TCAS transponder that transmitted their position to collision-avoidance systems on the ground and other aircraft and they became tragically invisible.[6]

The fundamental problem on that plane's flight management system—as well as on confusing drug labels or baffling street parking signs—has to do with providing too much information that doesn't actually *inform*. A pilot flying a plane, a driver looking for a parking space in New York, or a grandmother reaching for her pills: We're all looking for clear and comprehensible instructions to help us navigate a complex world. We need information, but what we're getting instead is *data*—untamed and unfiltered, without order, structure, or shape, and ultimately without meaning.

So how do we make sense of all that data, coming at us in ever greater amounts? As discussed in the last section, part of the challenge is a language issue—but only part. To achieve clarity, we also must apply design to information: We need to **organize, emphasize**, and **visualize**.

When dealing with complex and excessive information, one of the first orders of business is to sort through and prioritize that data—to establish, in design terms, "a hierarchy of information." This requires digging into the overall pile to extract the most meaningful information—figuring out what matters, and the order in which it matters. That will determine the organization and structure that's communicated in a label, an instruction manual, a billing statement, a website, or whatever media is used.

A big part of figuring out the structure is anticipating need. As Adler began work on her medicine labels, the first thing she did was put herself in the place of her grandparents. She even went through the motions of opening the medicine cabinet, sorting through the bottles, trying to find the right one. That gave her a real-world perspective that's often missing when communications are designed.

We see this lack of perspective in all kinds of documents coming from business and government. Take a recent edition of the official Medicare handbook, which promised, "Today's Medicare is about choice"—though it might as well say it's about confusion. Choice is touted as fundamentally good because it allows people to exercise free will. But too many choices and a lack of clear distinction between options is useless. The handbook is filled with government gobbledygook (including jargon such as "lifetime reserve days" and "durable medical equipment carrier"), but the main problem is structural: It doesn't orient the reader to the most basic workings of Medicare before launching into too many options and details.

And what's missing most is real-world context. People will not read the handbook as they would a novel. Instead they'll consult it as a question arises. Despite four pages of contents and topics, you cannot find something as simple as what to do if you lose your Medicare card. It is buried deep in a section titled "What is Medicare Part A?"

Similarly, when people consult their insurance policies, they're not looking for a leisurely read. Many homeowner's insurance policies are presented with claims procedures at the end of the document. In reality, most people only dig out their policies when they experience a loss. In that circumstance, they want to find claims information quickly—so a logical structure would put the claims information first, and highlight it.

If the structure of a document is intuitive for a reader, it's more likely to be read and understood. But you can also help guide people through structured information by arranging it into distinct, thematic, clearly marked sections or buckets. When people are confronted with information that isn't organized this way, "they're more likely to experience cognitive overload," says Neil Cohn, who teaches visual language at Tufts University. "Chunking is a way to make large amounts of information more digestible, and it's also a way to focus people's attention on certain things."[7]

Separate information into discrete ideas or steps; think sequentially; summarize longer material; hold back and de-emphasize less important information; get rid of what's unimportant. The last step may be the hardest for many, because the tendency is to want to overexplain and overinstruct.

One of the problems with most credit card agreements—aside from being absurdly long—is that there is no logical organization or chunking of the information in the agreement. As these agreements ballooned up to thirty pages of fine print, the conventional wisdom has become, "At this point, there's no going back—no way we could ever return to short, simple disclosures of yesteryear." When Elizabeth Warren began calling for shorter disclosures, the legal industry responded predictably: "A credit card product is inherently complex," Robert Cook, a partner at Hudson Cook, told *American Banker*. "It's never going to be a contract that is going to appear on one side of a piece of paper."[8]

Even as he was uttering those words, we'd already done it. Responding to President Obama's challenge to the credit card industry—to create a simple, easy-to-understand agreement that consumers would "not need a law degree or a magnifying glass to understand"—we decided to give it a try.

We consulted with consumer credit experts and contract lawyers, then brought together document designers and plain language writers. We studied dozens of credit card agreements from a wide range of providers and reviewed a seemingly impenetrable maze of complex federal and state regulations. And we knew going in that we'd have to find ways to eliminate 90 percent of what usually appears in a disclosure document. Inundation is disclosure's evil twin. So we knew, going in, that the gobbledygook would have to go.

We locked ourselves in a room and came up with a one-page, well-organized agreement (see Figure 5.2).

Working from a hybrid agreement, we laid in clear titles, easy-to-understand tables, and graphics showing basic price points, interest rates, and service fees. A big part of what makes this work is the use of design to create visual clarity. We dispensed with large amounts of data and zeroed in on seven key themes that could be chunked:

1. Use of card;
2. Credit limit;
3. Payment;
4. Interest;

5. Penalties;

6. Service fees;

7. Dispute resolution.

SIMPLIFIED CREDIT CARD AGREEMENT

This agreement is for your credit card account with us. It applies to you and all eligible users you approve. It starts when you first use your card and ends on the date printed on your card.

1 USE OF YOUR CARD
It can be used anywhere your card is accepted.

2 CREDIT LIMIT
Your credit limit is $5,000.00.
You may charge purchases and cash advances up to the credit limit shown on your monthly bill. We can increase, reduce, suspend, or cancel your credit limit at any time.

3 PAYMENT
We will bill you monthly for your purchases and cash advances, plus interest and other fees that may apply. You must pay at least the minimum monthly payment by the due date indicated on your bill. Paying more than the minimum balance will reduce your interest charges. Either of us can close this account at any time for any reason, but you will still owe all outstanding amounts.

4 INTEREST
At the end of each day, we will add new charges to your balance and subtract payments we receive and other credits that may apply. We will multiply the ending balance by the daily interest rate and add the interest charge to this balance. We will apply your payments to the balances with the highest interest rates first.

Your interest rates will be:

Purchases	Daily rate: 0.038%
	Annual rate: 13.90%
Cash Advance	Daily rate: 0.068%
	Annual rate: 24.90%
Balance Transfer	Daily rate: 0.038%
	Annual rate: 13.90%
Access Checks	Daily rate: 0.068%
	Annual rate: 24.90%

5 PENALTIES
If you don't follow the terms of this agreement, these penalties apply:

Late Payment	$39
Over Limit	$39
Returned Payment	$39

If you make 2 late payments within 6 months, we may notify you in advance that we are increasing your interest rate to the Late Payment rate. If you pay on time thereafter for 6 consecutive months, the rate will return to the previous rate.

| Late Payment rate | Annual rate: 29.40% |

6 SERVICE FEES
We may charge fees for various services:

Annual Fee	None
Cash Advance Fee	The greater of $10 or 3% of the amount
Foreign Transactions	The lesser of $2 or 1% of the US dollar amount

7 DISPUTE RESOLUTION
This agreement is governed by federal law and the laws of Delaware. If you think your bill is wrong, you must write to us within 60 days. We then have 90 days to resolve the error or explain why the bill is correct. Any dispute we cannot resolve will be decided by an independent arbitrator, whose decision is binding on us, but not on you. If you are not satisfied with the arbitrator's decision, you may then go to court.

More information
For an online version that explains this agreement and your privacy rights, visit www.bank.com/cardagreement. Or call us at 800-555-5555 for a written copy.

Written and designed by Siegel+Gale, pioneers in simplified communications

Figure 5.2

We sequenced that information logically (starting with basic use, ending up with potential problems/complications), and we used descriptive headings in bold type to provide cues for scanning and quick comprehension.

Virtually anything, no matter how complex, can be formatted this way—turned into a one- or two-page chunked document that immediately tells people what they need to know. *Wired* magazine recently did an interesting experiment in which they took one of the most complex and confusing forms of document known to man—the medical lab report—and turned it over to designers to see if it could be made readable.[9]

The results of this test were crystal clear—and you didn't have to be a lab technician to understand them. The designers took a sample blood test report that initially consisted of thirty measurements and more than four pages of fine print and distilled it down to a single page, chunked according to eight key measurements. The page used color boxes and bold headings to direct the eye to each important result. It focused on the most relevant numbers and summarized the more esoteric tests. The designers created an overview box at the top of the page headlined, "Your results at a glance." And at the bottom of the page, quite logically, the report told you what to conclude from this data ("What do your results mean?") and ended with a series of actionable steps ("What can you do?").

Let's take another example of a forbidding document: a standard apartment rental lease. Very few people actually read leases, but they ought to know what their rights are, right? A New York renters' group called Tenants & Neighbors came up with a creative way to bring more clarity to rental agreements by creating a simplified companion piece to leases—a set of "legal flash cards" that summarize all the critical issues covered in New York's official Tenant's Rights Guide (everything from security deposits to subletting). The cards employ the same design techniques you might use to clarify a document—creating summaries, separating and chunking information by themes, using color and icons—but with a fresh twist in terms of the format (see Figure 5.3). The pocket-sized cards are even more practical, from a user standpoint, than a one- or two-page document.

The same design strategies used to clarify a rental agreement can be applied to other complex documents—including instructions on how to use a smartphone. The "Out of the Box" simplified mobile phone, which was featured in a 2011 exhibit at the Museum of Modern Art, features an instruction manual specifically aimed at senior citizens. But the word "manual" doesn't fairly describe what designers Clara Gaggero and Adrian Westaway of Vitamins Design have done—they've actually created mobile phone packaging that doubles as an instruction manual and is intuitive even for non-techies. They understood that seniors often find learning new technologies frustrating, as they end up searching in the product box for help that isn't there.[10]

Figure 5.3   "Legal" flash cards help New York tenants understand their rights and responsibilities.

So Gaggero and Westaway responded with a box that is also a bound book, with the phone nestled inside. The new owner leafs through the pages of the book, gradually encountering both assembly instructions and various parts, all integrated within the bound book. (The designers also created a version of the phone that comes with instructional cards, one card per phone function, and a third model that presents instructions in a "map" format.)

We spoke to Adrian Westaway about this project, and he explained that when he and his design partners originally set out to create a simpler smartphone for older users, they assumed this would involve creating a stripped-down, Jitterbug-like phone with very few features. But their research with seniors found that people actually *wanted* all those features (the built-in camera, calculator, and so on). They didn't want to settle for less; they just wanted simpler, in terms of making it easy to understand and use all those features. And by relying on extensive up-close observation, Westaway's team also learned that seniors generally don't like to play with the product itself (the way a younger person might). They prefer to familiarize themselves with a new product in a more linear, step-by-step manner—which is why they responded so well to a phone nestled in the manual (see Figure 5.4).

Nothing beats an insurance policy for complexity. Insurance companies are loath to cut any information from policies, sometimes even when it's old and outdated. It is common practice for them to send policyholders amended pages and

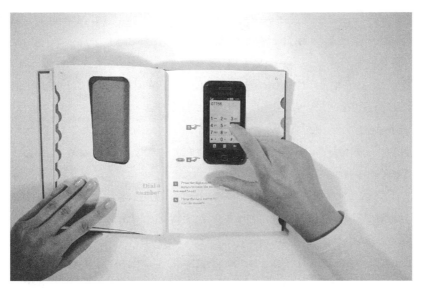

Figure 5.4   Phone is nestled within its instruction manual.

additions rather than a full revised policy. It's the reason why the policies grow to extraordinary lengths (and why no one reads them).

Which is why it stood out when major insurer ERGO, a Germany-based company with more than forty million customers worldwide, decided to take a stand against the clutter. ERGO recently introduced a new product series in which all the general insurance policies and statements have been reduced to what the company considers the bare minimum. A policy that used to be thirty pages full of general insurance standards has been reduced to two pages. The information is summarized and organized into logical and clearly marked sections, so that the entire policy is intended to be read and understood by someone in a matter of minutes.

ERGO is counting on "the simplicity paradox"—the less you tell people, the more they understand. They believe that when the policy was thirty pages, all the important information was buried. When everything was boiled down to two pages, people actually read it, got the key points, and are now more informed about their insurance.

According to Dr. David Stachon, ERGO's chief marketing officer, the impetus behind simplifying the insurance policies came out of field research. The company gathered all the routine data and research, but then sent a team out with video cameras and asked people what they thought about the insurance industry. ERGO learned that people didn't understand *anything* they were getting from their insurers—the companies were in effect talking to themselves. ERGO decided to seize the initiative by staking out a position as an insurance company that understood people and produced policies people could understand.

In offering greater clarity to customers, ERGO also brought clarity to its own operation and mission. The company's simplicity initiative is having a significant impact *inside* the corporate culture, Stachon notes. "I've been with the company for years, and never have I seen such an activity and excitement level," he says. "Many people here feel that there have been shortcomings in understandability in the past in this industry—and most are very happy to tackle this problem."[11]

In boiling its insurance policy down to two pages, ERGO had to decide: What should be emphasized? Streamlining and summarizing are the first steps in emphasizing what's important. But design elements—highlighting, type size, boldface, color—can also be used to create emphasis. One of the cardinal sins of fine print (aside from being just too damn small) is that there is often no use of design elements to create emphasis. Everything blends together in a sea of gray and the eye has nothing to focus on. If everything is emphasized, there is no emphasis.

Just look at the before-and-after pages from a typical loan agreement—the problem is, in the "before" you don't know where to look. In the sample shown in Figure 5.5, poor alignment results in items fighting each other for your attention. By creating distinctive subject headings that flow smoothly and logically, you create a path for the reader to follow. And along that path, occasional cues help people figure out what to pay special attention to (through the use of small flags like "Important" and "Action Required"). The sequence of topics anticipates the readers' unfamiliarity with loan agreements and relates the provisions to real-world circumstances.

Keep in mind that every change in size, style, position, or alignment of type on a page indicates a shift in emphasis and implies meaning, whether intended or not. Generally, try to limit types to no more than three sizes or weights per page. And use bold or italic for emphasis without overusing them. You don't want to use design elements willy-nilly—overemphasis

Simple

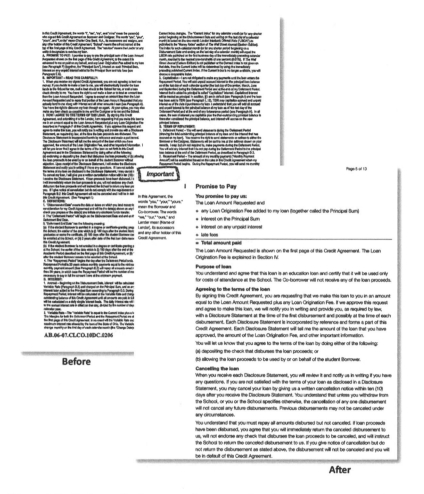

Figure 5.5   Before and after pages from a student loan agreement. The latter takes prose and presents it as an equation to make the calculations clear.

122

(for instance, **ALL BOLD CAPS**) can end up being no more helpful than underemphasis, and a lot more annoying.

To achieve clarity in communications with customers, marketing instincts to oversell must be restrained (in the same way that the legal instinct to "cover all risks" must be tempered). One of the best examples of this can be seen in packaging, where clarity is achieved through a disciplined focus on what's important to the customer. In packaging (and in ads, documents, and various forms of communication), "white space" can be one of the most critical design elements because it helps people focus.

It's no accident that Apple's packaging and ads feature mostly white space. "There is tremendous power in all that white space," says the brand's longtime ad director.

Packaging that uses a simple design aesthetic with lots of white space stands out in a crowded, visually chaotic marketplace. Instead of having a laundry list of features and benefits, such packaging "allows the consumer to project attributes and their own personal interpretations on a blank canvas," says designer Rob Wallace.[12] Lee Clow, the TBWA ad chief who has worked on Apple's marketing for years, says the brand uses white space on packaging and ads to reinforce the sense of clarity and simplicity associated with its products. Clow says that packaging is the first signal to people that the entire experience will be clean, clear, and elegant.[13]

This isn't just a matter of aesthetics. Clarity can make or break the sale when someone is in the store trying to make sense of packaging. Nestlé's Amanda Bach cites the "four-second rule," meaning you have about four seconds, at most, to hold people's attention with your packaging. If you overwhelm or confuse them, they're on to the next product. Simpler packaging is more inviting and helps people more easily locate specific information they may be looking for. By Bach's formula, "Clutter equals confusion equals harried shopper," while "Simplicity equals clarity equals satisfied shopper."[14]

One reason white space is effective is that it is anti-data. But we can't always just get rid of information (nor would we wish to). However we can, at times, show rather than just tell.

The appeal of visualization is rooted in biology. The brain simply processes images better than words, devoting more than half its processing power to this task. According to Colin Ware, who directs the Data Visualization Lab at the University of New Hampshire, the human eye tends to seek out and focus on visual stimuli that are easy to recognize and separate from the rest of the clutter—including color, shapes, and patterns.[15]

Data visualization (or "data viz," as it's sometimes called) makes it possible to take even the most complex concepts and distill them down to a dynamic image; a fifty-page document replete with charts and graphs can be summarized in one web screen. Moreover, visualization is engaging because it invites the viewer to interpret the images, fill in gaps, and draw conclusions that aren't necessarily spelled out.

At the same time, visualization can take a concept that's somewhat abstract when explained in words and make it more real and understandable. To bring more clarity to the concept that "Paying your credit card bill over time costs you more than paying in full," we used the power of information design. A series of dinner plates shows how one purchase made with a credit card grows in cost depending upon when you pay for it (see Figure 5.6a).

Similarly, the graphic shown in Figure 5.6b focuses on the total credit card balance rather than one transaction, and shows how paying $106 more per month cuts repayment time by eleven years, six months.

Visualization is a relatively new but extremely important simplification tool because it can be used to provide context, show cause-and-effect relationships, and reveal anomalies and trends—the kind of complex information that might otherwise require mountains of explicatory data. The famous information designer Hans Rosling, founder of Gapminder, uses visualization to provide a snapshot of long-term global trends in income inequality and mortality rates. As the *New York Times* noted, instead of swamping us with "yawn-inducing numbers on gross domestic product per capita," Rosling's animated graphics

A $62 dinner could cost you:

Figure 5.6a

**Paying off your current balance
of $9,811.31 will require:**

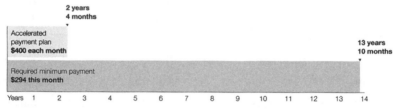

Figure 5.6b

convey all you need to know with simple bubbles (representing each country) that grow or shrink, and rise or fall, over time.[16]

> "Clutter and confusion are failures of design, not attributes of information."
>
> —EDWARD TUFTE

Bob Greenberg, who runs the digital marketing agency R/GA, predicts that "data visualization is one of the 'next big things' of the digital age, equally important to consumers and companies." (And we'd add governments, which could make great use of data viz to help inform the public on complex issues.) Greenberg cites financial services as one business where consumers will soon expect visualization "as a given." He notes that already, companies such as Mint.com allow users "to view their financial data in real time, aggregating content from multiple financial accounts. Not only can users view their own data, but they can compare their financial habits to others in the same city, state or country."[17]

Healthcare is another area where visualization could play a huge role. Information on health can be hard for people to grasp when it's presented as cold facts and statistics. (What does it really mean, in practical terms, if a medication increases your risk of illness by 17 percent but simultaneously has a six in one thousand chance of a certain side effect?) To make the numbers more real and clear, a group of doctors based at the David Geffen School of Medicine at UCLA recently created a "medical dartboard" to visualize the health risks associated with certain procedures (see Figure 5.7). Why a dartboard? "Most people have little trouble with the concept that the result of throwing a dart would be proportional to the areas on a board that provide a good reward or bad one," the doctors wrote in the journal *PLoS Medicine*.[18]

Promising as it is, visualization won't necessarily save us from gobbledygook. The U.S. Patent Office created a "dashboard" with an inviting, highly visual interface that uses cockpit-style gauges to illustrate data (a step in the right direction). But no one seems to have paused to reflect on what the gauges measure: "first action office pendency," "traditional total pendency," "actions per

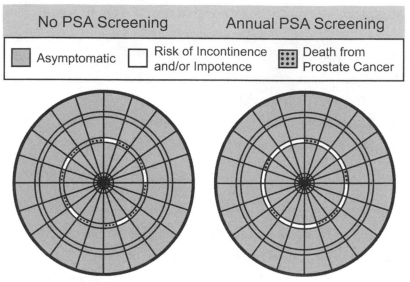

Figure 5.7

disposal," and so on. By bogging down the visuals with clunky language, they managed to make a pretty intuitive activity—applying for a patent—sound mysterious and otherworldly.

And all you need do is look at the typical PowerPoint presentation to understand that good visualization is dependent on the same human qualities as other forms of communication—a thoughtful approach to the subject, strong organization of ideas, concise and clear expression of those ideas. Lacking that, one visual slide can become as gobbledygooked up as ten pages of fine print. And it can be so thoroughly confusing and demoralizing that it can bring even the powerful U.S. military to the point of surrender.

A couple of years back, a PowerPoint slide—a quagmire of words, circles, and arrows that purportedly depicted the military situation in Afghanistan—became notorious as quite possibly one of the most complex images ever produced. The general overseeing Afghan operations at the time, Stanley A. McChrystal, reportedly took a long hard look at the image and concluded, "When we understand this slide, we'll have won the war."[19]

Design and visualization can only do so much. The rest depends on clarity of language. And to be clear, words should be plain.

Today, we are drowning in legalese, "corporate-speak," and other forms of jargon we can't understand. It comes at us in tidal waves of fine print we can't (or simply won't) read. And yet we have pressing business to conduct, lives to lead, songs to hear—so we agree to anything and everything in the fine print.

And the more we go along with it, the worse the problem gets. Credit card agreements are now twenty times as long as they were in 1980. As consumer advocate Elizabeth Warren points out, the old agreements "told you the interest rate, about being late, and that was pretty much it."

"Plain language is a civil right."
—Al Gore

So why the need for all the extra pages? Because, as Warren explains, "that's where the tricks and traps are."[20]

Even routine phone bills are filled with arcane and often

misleading terms. You've probably received a bill at some point telling you about an unavoidable hike in the "Carrier Cost Recovery Fee." That sounds "governmental," but it's just a made-up name for a fee that is passing along the cost of doing business. And since so many unintelligible fees and charges appear on the phone bill already, it's easy to slip in yet another.

So what's going on here? Has everything just gotten so complicated—with so many unavoidable terms and conditions—that there's no way to express things simply anymore? That's what some would have you believe. But the plain truth is this: Increasingly, people in business and government are using language for a purpose other than clear communication. They're using it to conceal, muddle, confuse, and obfuscate.

The roots of a movement

Through the years, the simplicity movement has been, first and foremost, a language movement, aimed primarily at governmental, corporate, and legal jargon. It gained momentum in the mid-1970s, after the Vietnam War and the Watergate scandal—when Americans were no longer willing to take official language at face value. The consumer movement also was growing at this time. People demanded more information about products, more user-friendly forms, readable regulations, and clear communications from the public and private institutions they had come to distrust.

In these early days of the "plain English" or "plain language" movement, our firm was at the eye of the storm—helping to advance New York's groundbreaking plain English law in 1977 and working on one of the first language simplification projects in the federal government during the Carter administration. It was Jimmy Carter—love him or hate him—who emerged as an early champion of simplification. He signed a landmark 1978 executive order directing federal officials to ensure that regulations be "written in plain English and understandable to those who must comply with it." Carter oversaw ambitious efforts to help agencies write simple regulations and documents, while also initiating efforts to simplify tax forms and instructions.

> The term "gobbledygook" was coined in 1944 by a Texas congressman appropriately named Maury Maverick, who used it to describe the bureaucratic jargon he encountered while overseeing a wartime government agency. In a memo to staffers, Maverick wrote, "Stay off the gobbledygook. It only fouls people up. For Lord's sake, be short and say what you're talking about.... Anyone using the words 'activation' or 'implementation' will be shot."[21]

So what came next? Ronald Reagan. In 1981, President Reagan rescinded all plain English orders (though his administration did agree to fund the IRS 1040EZ tax form). To Reagan and other critics, plain language initiatives were just another "regulation"—one more nitpicking rule being forced upon the free market. The plain language movement rebounded somewhat in 1998 when President Clinton issued a memorandum calling for executive departments and agencies to use plain English in all government documents. Clinton's vice president, Al Gore, oversaw government plain English training programs and presented the "No Gobbledygook" awards monthly to federal employees who took bureaucratic messages and turned them into plain language. It was Gore who famously declared, "Plain language is a civil right."

Fast-forward through the George W. Bush years—the folksy president showed no interest in plain language as a larger concept—and we come to the most recent manifestation of the movement, Obama's signing of the Plain Writing Act of 2010. The law requires that government documents be written in "plain language," defined as writing that is "clear, concise, well-organized."

Carter, Clinton, Gore, Obama: With so many of the world's most powerful and influential leaders championing plain language, why hasn't there been more progress? Part of the answer may be that the issue became overly politicized. Simplification and plain language shouldn't be a left/right issue—everyone, including business, benefits from clearer communication. But the bigger issue may be that it's hard to legislate simplicity. Attempts to do so can end up fostering complexity. For example, current plain language laws have differing compliance

Clarify

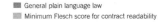

Figure 5.8   In the United States today, plain language laws vary from state to state, as illustrated in this Siegel+Gale sketch.

requirements from state to state and even from one industry to the next.

Ironically, when laws promoting simplicity and clarity are overly prescriptive and specific, they can have a perverse effect—efforts to comply are turned over to company lawyers, who focus on adhering to the letter of the law rather than the spirit of it. And so we end up with thirty-page disclosure documents that technically comply with the law but are even more impenetrable than before. When it comes to simplicity, regulations should be written in terms of general objectives rather than as a set of detailed rules, mandated statements, and readability formulas. They should set the goal, not dictate the path.

The business incentive: why plain pays off

> *"Most of the quarterly filings, prospectuses, annual reports and other editorial output of corporate America are dense and confusing. Most of it, I suspect, gets tossed into the garbage unread."*[22]
>
> —ARTHUR LEVITT,
> FORMER SEC CHAIR

When plain language is seen as just another regulation or legal requirement, the primary concern of business becomes compliance, not communication. But when companies look at this differently—as a better way of doing business—they're more apt to make a sincere and full-scale effort to actually simplify and improve communications with customers.

Why should companies embrace plain language on their own? For both moral and practical reasons, but let's start with the practical.

When companies communicate simply and honestly with customers, the result is:

- Distinctive added value to products and services;
- Customers who are more satisfied and better informed, resulting in...

- A higher level of trust: Our research found that 84 percent of consumers are more likely to trust a company that uses jargon-free plain English;[23]
- Greater brand loyalty stemming from that increased trust.

Simple language yields "cognitive fluency"—a term used by psychologists as a measure of how easy it is to think about something. When we encounter words and concepts that are easy to understand, we become more accepting, more trusting. As cognitive fluency expert Daniel Oppenheimer explained to us, "Engaging with things that are fluent is an inherently positive experience, much like eating chocolate or playing with a puppy." So, short of handing out sweets or pups, plain language is an easy way to make your customers feel good.

At the same time, it's a way to feel good about your business and yourself. Beyond the business reasons, plain speaking is the right thing to do. This isn't just about improving bottom lines. It's about achieving our highest ideals. When a company is known for being straightforward and honest in all its dealings with the public, it engenders a sense of purpose and pride. It can help remind people in business why they got in that business in the first place.

So there's the ideal. Now let's consider the present-day reality. Even with all these good reasons to speak plainly and clearly, the level of gobbledygook in business has continued to rise. As the *Wall Street Journal* recently reported, business schools are trying to address the problem by adding crash courses on writing and speaking clearly, because companies are complaining that too many grads arrive full of B-school jargon.[24] It can be counterproductive inside the company. Unclear language makes it harder to articulate strategies and ideas with precision. But worse than that, when people inside a company constantly talk to each other in their own language, it naturally seeps out to the world at large.

It finds its way to the company's investors. Our surveys have found that most investors (65 percent) consider investment prospectuses to be extremely difficult to understand. As a result, many investors choose not to read investment materials. And it's hard to blame them when they're confronted with writing like this, from a prospectus issued by the film studio Lionsgate:

> The registrant hereby amends this registration statement on such date or dates as may be necessary to delay its effective date until the registrant shall file a further amendment which specifically states that this registration statement shall thereafter become effective in accordance with Section 8(a) of the Securities Act, or until the registration statement shall become effective on such date as the Securities and Exchange Commission, acting pursuant to said Section 8(a), may determine.[25]

If that sentence were a Lionsgate film, it would be classified as a tragicomedy.

Of course it's one thing when jargon finds its way into financial reports and papers—we've come to expect financial types to talk in that cryptic language known as "Finglish." But it can be even more disconcerting to see jargon take over everyday correspondence with customers—through phone bills, cable bills, letters from the utility company, product instruction manuals, loan applications, and more.

On a phone bill, "current charges" is confusing because the bill includes charges for one month in advance—to the rest of us, that is "future," not "current." It's just one example of a company speaking to itself; a subsequent section, talking about "full-month credits" for "partial-month discounts," is even more confusing.

It might seem that learning to speak plainly would be easy for business to learn. But the hard part is breaking the habit and custom of "talking like a company." People in business have been trained to adopt a certain voice, tone, and vocabulary that suggests, *I'm part of a buttoned-down corporate world where everything is done according to strict policy. I represent a large, faceless business entity; you are a small, powerless customer. Let's proceed from there.*

One of the most important things companies can do to bring more clarity to their communication is to abandon this impersonal, overly formal style and adopt a much more "human" approach to communications. Warren Buffett takes

> *"The secret to more effective writing is simple:* talk *to your reader. Pretend the person who'll read your letter or report is sitting across from you. Be informal. Relax."*
>
> —RUDOLF FLESCH, AUTHOR OF *SAY WHAT YOU MEAN*

this approach when he writes the famed Berkshire Hathaway annual report. When composing the report, Buffett explained once in a letter, "I picture my sisters—highly intelligent, but not experts in accounting or finance. They will understand plain English, but jargon may puzzle them. My goal is to give the information I would wish to receive if our positions were reversed."[26]

While Buffett pictures his sisters, Arthur Levitt, the former SEC chairman (who presided over a plain English initiative during his tenure at the commission), told the publication *Government Executive* that when trying to figure out if something is understandable, "I think of my Aunt Edna. Can Aunt Edna understand it? If she can't, you've got to rewrite it."[27]

Aunt Edna would likely respond to the same things most of us do:

- Short sentences.
- Simple, everyday words in place of jargon or technical terms. (When it is necessary to use technical terms, provide explanation and examples.)
- The use of personal pronouns such as "I" and "you."

- Active rather than passive verbs.
- And—as an added touch—humor, grace, or anything to break the tedium.

Part of learning to speak clearly as a company is finding a company's own distinctive and authentic voice—not the "official" (and often officious) voice of a generic corporation, but the voice that expresses the ideals and personality of the brand, the company, and all the human beings behind it. That voice should come through clearly in all communications, at all points of contact with customers. Employees should be taught and encouraged to speak with consumers in a way that's direct, transparent, straightforward, and human. Whether on the company blog, in the office, or on the sales floor, they should have the freedom to express *their* personalities as well as the personality associated with the brand.

Look at how the personality of Apple is expressed in this set of guidelines for apps sold at the App Store.

> We have over 250,000 apps in the App Store. We don't need any more Fart apps. If your app doesn't do something useful or provide some form of lasting entertainment, it may not be accepted.

As the *Financial Times* columnist Lucy Kellaway noted, "The tone is direct, comic and elegantly threatening.... I found myself reading it effortlessly, even though I barely know what an 'app' is."[28]

We found this same level of "humanness" to be present in a recent exchange we had with iTunes customer service involving a botched movie download. The response took a conversational tone, repeatedly addressed the customer personally by name, showed a clear understanding of the specifics of the problem being discussed, offered simple and practical solutions, and even provided useful tips to avoid future problems— it had the feeling of a conversation more than a rote reply, and in general was a model for clear, engaging communication with customers (see Figure 5.9).

Let's face it, glitches in service and malfunctions in products are going to happen—but companies can control the way they talk to people about these matters, and it does make a big difference. No one would deny that Netflix messed up big-time last year when the company tried to rush through a major price hike and structural change in its DVD rental offering. But one thing Netflix got *right* was the apology—which is a good example of how plain English is the only way to talk when you're in a jam. Netflix CEO Reed Hastings sent an email to customers that began with the lines:

> *Dear [Name],*
> *I messed up. I owe you an explanation.*

That candid admission alone is almost enough to make you want to forgive Hastings right away. But the letter also goes

Clarify

Amazing email exchange with iTunes customer service conveys personal, engaging communication.

Nice unsolicited follow-up email from iTunes

Irene Etzkorn

From:	iTunes Store <iTunesStoreSupport@apple.com>
Sent:	Sunday, July 31, 2011 1:11 PM
To:	Irene Etzkorn
Subject:	Re: My concern isn't listed here; Follow-up: 162423973

Follow-Up: 162423973 — Conversational tone

Hello again, — Followed up to ensure satisfaction

I wanted to send a quick note to see if you are still experiencing any difficulties with the iTunes Store. Resolving your issue is important to me, so please don't hesitate to reply if you need any further assistance.

Sincerely,

Raghunath
iTunes Store/Mac App Store Customer Support

Tells me when he is there to further personal connection.

Please Note: I work Saturday to Wednesday, 7 AM to 4 PM CST

Thank you for allowing me the opportunity to assist you.

Dear Irene, — Immediately identifies himself and establishes personal rapport

My name is Raghunath and I am an advisor with iTunes store support team. Before I begin addressing your mail, I would like to apologize for the delay in responding to your inquiry. This is certainly not the customary wait time for a reply from the iTunes Store Customer Support. — I hadn't noticed they were slow to respond. Nice pre-emptive strike.

We have been experiencing higher volumes than expected, and your patience is greatly appreciated. — Specific mention of my problem

I understand that you ran int a bit of trouble with the movie "Morning Glory" which you rented from the iTunes store. Not to worry, I'm sure that you are looking forward to having this resolved, and I will gladly do everything I can to assist.

— Uses my first name.

Irene, I have issued a refund for this rental. In five to seven business days, you will see a refund of $4.99 posted to the card that was used for this purchase. — Clear, specific action.

I highly recommend renting and downloading large files, such as movie rentals, to a computer then syncing it your iPad to watch. Sometimes Wi-Fi or your ISPs network can be unreliable, which can result in items not downloading properly or at all. — Useful tip for future downloads.

Irene, I hope this resolves your issue. If you require further assistance, please do not hesitate to reply to this email and I will be more than happy to assist you further.

Thank you for being an iTunes Store customer.

Have a nice day!

Sincerely,

Raghunath
iTunes Store/Mac App Store Customer Support

1

Original response from iTunes.

Figure 5.9   Email exchange between the author and iTunes customer support.

141

on to explain the misstep in very personal, human, and emotional terms. (At one point Hasting confesses that his "greatest fear" was that he'd move too slowly in shifting from DVDs to streaming; this may help customers understand why he ended up moving too quickly.) And then Hastings transitions from apology to remedial action in a no-nonsense way: "So here is what we are doing and why."

Looking at this letter, we'd swear Hastings got a peek at one of our research reports, which showed that the best way to present bad news is with clarity and honesty. This goes against everything corporate lawyers and PR types teach— that if you get in a jam, try to "spin" your way out of it. It doesn't work: People want straight talk, *especially* in troubled times. In fact, if companies deliver bad news honestly and clearly, we found that they can actually *strengthen* customer relationships—and lay the foundation for increased trust when conditions improve.

Perhaps the biggest challenge when adopting plain language is overcoming the resistance to it within corporate culture. People will tell you, "This is business—you can't say that!" Lawyers, in particular, will tell you this.

Many corporate lawyers attack plain English without understanding what it's about. Too many see it in simplistic terms. They ignore the clear evidence that most legal documents can be simplified without sacrificing their legal force or encouraging litigation; they maintain that legalese is more precise than plain English. But a business doesn't have to give up legal protections in order to simplify. Whatever protections,

> *"The finest language is mostly made up of simple unimposing words."*
>
> —GEORGE ELIOT

rights, or remedies a corporation wants to assert can still be put in writing—just put them in terms understandable to the consumer. That can actually end up putting you on safer legal ground, because it provides plain evidence that you were never trying to hide anything or hoodwink anyone.

Such logic notwithstanding, complexity and legalese are so entrenched in many companies that if you try to simplify anything, someone is bound to tell you it can't be done. At this point, it becomes necessary to, in the words of Nietzsche, "philosophize with a hammer"—to smash the idols and defy the conventions of business protocol. Sometimes the only way to convince people that things can be simplified is just to go ahead and simplify them.

And if Nietzsche doesn't provide enough inspiration, turn to Aristotle, who laid out a classic model for clear communications built around *logos*, *pathos*, and *ethos*. In Aristotle's classical theory of persuasion, or "rhetorical theory," he (rather persuasively) cites three examples of "proofs" (principles of persuasion) to make your message hit home.

1. **Logos:** logic and reason (embedded in the language itself)
2. **Pathos:** emotional appeal (directed toward the audience)
3. **Ethos:** character and credibility (centered with the speaker)

To return to the context of modern business, we point to Warren Buffett's annual letter to Berkshire Hathaway shareholders. In 2009, a year following hellish economic turmoil, Buffett wrote to his shareholders with clarity, respect, and at eye level—three things that seem absent in the rest of the financial world. Buffett's exemplification of Aristotle's principles of rhetorical theory is spot on and apparent within his first few pages.

1. **Logos:** Buffett clearly explains the rationale behind using an S&P 500 yardstick to measure Berkshire Hathaway's performance:

   Our metrics for evaluating our managerial performance are displayed on the facing page. From the start, Charlie and I have believed in having a rational and unbending standard for measuring what we have—or have not—accomplished. That keeps us from the temptation of seeing where the arrow of performance lands and then painting the bull's eye around it.

   Selecting the S&P 500 as our bogey was an easy choice because our shareholders, at virtually no cost, can match its performance by holding an index fund. Why should they pay us for merely duplicating that result?

2. **Pathos:** Buffett speaks to all members of his potential audience and casts a wide net of appeal by referencing a mathematician and country music in a couple of sentences:

   > *Jacobi, the great Prussian mathematician,... counseled "Invert, always invert" as an aid to solving difficult problems. (I can report as well that this inversion approach works on a less lofty level: Sing a country song in reverse, and you will quickly recover your car, house and wife.)*

   With unusual relatability for such a lofty financial power, Buffett gives the reader a peek behind the curtain with a personal and folksy tone. Rather than the vice chairman and CEO, it's "Charlie and I."

3. **Ethos:** Buffett has this in spades. Not only is he the CEO of the company, but he's also a financial genius. You don't garner nicknames like "the Oracle of Omaha" without some credibility.

Using *logos*, *pathos*, and *ethos*, Buffett keeps the lofty language and confusing concepts in check, his audience in mind, and his character on display. In fact, the Berkshire Hathaway annual

> *"More important than the quest for certainty is the quest for clarity."*
> —FRANÇOIS GAUTIER

shareholders' letter is such a smart piece of corporate communications that shareholders and nonshareholders alike look forward to it each February.

It could be argued that Aristotle's classic approach applies to corporate communications in general. The combination of *logos* (to ensure that logic and common sense prevail in all your messaging), *pathos* (empathizing with and relating to your customers), and *ethos* (maintaining integrity, honesty, and transparency in your interactions with customers) provides a model that is solid—so solid, in fact, that it has held up for a couple of thousand years.

Many people think that by using overblown language in their reports or writings they will appear to be "smarter." But Princeton professor Daniel Oppenheimer tested this by manipulating the complexity of pieces of writing to see how readers judged the intelligence of authors. The result? As the text became more complicated, readers gave a *lower* estimate of the author's intelligence.[29]

PART III

Simplicity Spreads

CHAPTER 6

Top-Down and Bottom-Up

How Complex Organizations Simplify

IT'S NEVER BEEN MORE CRITICAL FOR COMPANIES
TO SIMPLIFY. TO DO SO REQUIRES A COMMIT-
MENT FROM THE TOP, CLARITY OF PURPOSE, AND
A "CULTURE OF SIMPLICITY" THAT PERMEATES
THE ENTIRE ORGANIZATION.

Can a company transform itself so that simplicity becomes part
of its DNA?

A few years ago, we were invited to an event in New York
that, considering our area of specialty, felt a little bit like step-
ping into heaven—billowing white curtains, luxurious white
sofas, white carpeting, with everyone dressed in white and
talking about the virtues of simplicity. We even met someone
who had the title of "chief simplicity officer." In this case, the
pearly gates had a sign saying, "The Simplicity Event."[1]

It was sponsored by Philips and was intended to unveil

> *"Great leaders are almost always great simplifiers, who can cut through argument, debate, and doubt to offer a solution everybody can understand."*
> —GENERAL COLIN POWELL

the company's cultural transformation from an R&D-driven to a customer-centric one with a singular focus on simplicity. For a global technology powerhouse filing three thousand patents a year, complexity is a fact of life. But Philips' CEO, Gerard Kleisterlee, wanted to change the company in a fundamental way. His management team set out to find a relevant, competitive positioning that would both unite and distinguish a company that makes electronics as diverse as fryers and magnetic resonance imaging machines. Finally, a comment made in jest by one of the executives—"A day when everything was simple at Philips: That would be a point of difference"—became the rallying cry. Because it was so far from reality at the time, it was a source of both inspiration and anxiety.

The company's executive committee took a year to investigate how the market would react to the new positioning and to evaluate the magnitude of the change. Canvassing 1,650 consumers and 180 corporate customers in eight countries, Philips asked them to identify big societal issues the company should address. Sure enough, overwhelming complexity and fear of technology were cited. Confident that they had tapped into a universal need, Philips began developing their response.

Thus began a multifaceted, widespread, and ongoing systematic transformation of products and processes throughout the company. Finance, Design, Marketing, Communications, Human Resources—every area of the company—adopted a simple set of guiding pillars:

- Designed around you
- Easy to use
- Advanced

At the Simplicity Event, Philips was already showing the impact of its new philosophy on future products in the prototype stages. The common denominator in all of them was ease of use and simplicity of design. Why repaint a wall to test a new paint color? Instead, hold a paint chip to a sensor on a lamp that prompts the lightbulb to customize the light, and watch the room magically change color. And as for those impossible remote controls? In Philips' vision of a simpler world, the button-filled remote has been replaced by a wand with a single button that still achieves all functions. The basic need to leave household reminders has been handled by a touch-sensitive, wall-hung message board where one writes freehand and then touches the photo of a family member to send a note.

The product design changes were only the beginning. Upon talking to the man in charge, Chief Marketing Officer Andrea Ragnetti, we learned that the simplicity initiative extended into all areas of the company. Recruiting a new employee used to drag on for two months—now it took a week. PowerPoint presentations would consume hours—now there is a ten-slide limit (literally cutting "a billion slides a year"). In terms of corporate structure, thirteen divisions have been reduced to five. Financial reports have been rewritten and reformatted to make them more understandable and actionable.

And from the standpoint of its customers, Philips has expanded the boundaries of what simplicity means. They've defined it as removing any nuisance or hindrance in people's lives. The company's mission now is to actively look for all the burrs under the saddle in our daily lives, and to apply its vast know-how and resources to try to remove them.

It's an ambitious goal, and the jury's still out on whether Philips will pull it off, but there's no doubt that the company is providing a useful model on corporate-wide simplification. The first thing Philips did right—and this is a universal lesson that should be heeded by any company seeking to imbue its culture with a simplicity mindset—is that it established support for simplification at the top of the company. That a high-level exec like CMO Ragnetti was given sole responsibility for the effort sent the signal that simplification was to be a serious company-wide effort. In case employees somehow missed that signal, Philips began surveying all employees twice a year to make sure they understood and were on board with the brand promise. (Most were; in fact, it was the employees who quickly generated a list of five hundred "Simplicity Proof Points," suggested changes that could be implemented quickly as part of the makeover.)

Meanwhile, the company went public with its simplicity promise at the New York event and beyond, with a major marketing campaign under the banner of "Sense and Simplicity." Ragnetti believed that by making this bold public statement, the company would be under pressure to live up to the mission and transform itself quickly. Jasper van Kuijk of TU Delft, who has studied Philips and consulted with the company on research projects, observes that when it came to trying to simplify itself, "Philips took a top-down approach. They started with the management and the big picture and said, 'Simplicity is important to us.' But they also took an 'outside in' approach by coming up with a 'sense and simplicity' campaign that signaled to people, 'This is what we value; this is what we're about now.'"

In the preceding chapters, we noted that simplicity is a product of continuous attempts to empathize, distill, and clarify. When done on a project-by-project basis, this can result in the creation of an isolated product or service that is simpler. But the real challenge is to be able to apply these principles on a consistent basis throughout an organization. This is simplification on a higher plane. When it's done right, a company and its culture are imbued with an ethos that ensures every action, process, and decision will be judged through the lens of simplicity.

> *"Don't make the process harder than it is."*
>
> —JACK WELCH

How does this kind of transformation begin? Better to ask *where* it must begin—and the answer is, "At the top." In almost every instance where we've seen companies become successful simplifiers, strong senior-level executives have led the effort by making a deep, unwavering commitment to institutional simplicity. It comes down to this: When top management believes in simplicity and clarity and won't tolerate deviations from those beliefs, employees cannot hide behind bureaucracy or use jargon as a shield. Conversely, if those in charge don't establish that clarity is the expectation, employees may tend to take the easier path of complexity.

Why CEOs are stymied by complexity

It's easy to say that top executives should champion simplicity. However, the truth is that many CEOs are well aware of the business challenge brought on by complexity—yet don't know how to get their arms around that challenge. IBM completed a global study of more than fifteen hundred CEOs and found that most business leaders surveyed believe escalating complexity is *the* biggest challenge facing them. At the same time, IBM's researchers uncovered what they called a "complexity gap"—while eight in ten CEOs expect their environment to grow increasingly complex, less than half of them know how to deal with this problem.[2]

They'd better figure it out, because a separate study, by the Warwick Business School, indicates that complexity is exacting heavy tolls on companies. The Warwick study looked at the two hundred largest companies in the world and found they were wasting an average of 10 percent of annual profits—over a billion dollars a year—as a result of overly complex processes, bloated product portfolios, and increasing management layers. (The study revealed that it was not uncommon to find as many as *sixteen* layers of management in the most complex companies.)

Such organizational complexity is a natural by-product of growth and expansion, acquisitions, and diversification. Simon Collinson, one of the authors of the Warwick study, noted that "companies that try to do too much, or spread themselves too thin across markets" often fall prey to corporate complexity. Another problem cited is that people within these companies "over-engineer everything to justify their existence."[3]

In sharp contrast, Apple's laser-sharp focus keeps its product line streamlined and manageable. Steve Jobs once remarked that Apple's success was due in large part to "saying no to 1,000 things to make sure we don't get on the wrong track or try to do too much." He added, "We're always thinking about new markets we could enter, but it's only by saying no that you can concentrate on the things that are really important."[4]

> *"We have one hardware organization. We have one software organization. It's not like we're this big company with all these divisions that are cranking out products. We're simpletons."*[5]
>
> —Tim Cook, current CEO, Apple

Jobs understood that companies without a sharp focus fall prey to distraction, confusion, dilution of quality, and even paralysis. They lose sight of essential priorities, get tangled up in their own layers of bureaucracy, lose touch with the marketplace. Sometimes they even lose track of their own products and models.

So how can business leaders guide their companies away from the pitfalls of complexity? The IBM study (with chief executive officers worldwide) concluded that "creative leadership" is necessary—manifesting itself in taking bold actions to restructure organizations and processes with an eye toward simplification, while reinventing customer relationships with a greater focus on understanding and serving customer needs. Among the study's findings:

The most successful organizations co-create products and services with customers, and integrate customers into core processes. They are adopting new channels to engage and stay in tune with customers. By drawing more insight from the available data, successful CEOs make customer intimacy their number-one priority.

Better performers manage complexity on behalf of their organizations, customers and partners. They do so by simplifying operations and products, and increasing dexterity to change the way they work, access resources and enter markets around the world. Compared to other CEOs, dexterous leaders expect 20 percent more future revenue to come from new sources.

In terms of how you manage complexity in a company, we think it can be broken down into several concrete steps.

The first thing top executives must do is take charge of—and full responsibility for—the whole issue of simplification. Too many company leaders have either ignored the issue or left it to middle management. Indeed, we think part of the complexity crisis in business can be traced to the rise of middle management that occurred as large numbers of companies downsized radically in 2003 and again in 2008. At the time, many middle managers suddenly were given more responsibility for setting policy, determining processes, even defining corporate missions. But middle managers (having had leadership thrust upon them, instead of earning it) are rarely bold enough to shake the status quo, preferring instead to rely on incremental change—which often involves amending, extending, and all the other sins that foster complexity. Case in point: Brand managers need to justify their existence, which means that once a product or service is launched, they're under pressure to expand market share—not so much by innovating as by incrementally adding on, segmenting, and proliferating new models of old offerings.

We've found that among executives and managers, the lower the position in the company, the higher the resistance to innovation (and thereby the innovative approaches required for simplification). Among middle managers, conversations tend to focus on "why we can't do that."

That's why it's imperative that top-level executives declare unequivocally, "We *can* do this—and in fact, we must." And perhaps the best place to start is with simplification and clarification of a company's mission and its guiding principles.

A simple purpose

Over time, a company purpose can become muddled and clouded by complexity. With this in mind, a number of companies that are successful simplifiers have started by distilling the mission statement down to its essence. For example:

- **JetBlue.** The airline recently reviewed its best practices and strategy—which had ballooned to twenty-three objectives. That was distilled so that "23 became 14, and then 10, and we crystallized them into two— culture and offerings," chief executive David Barger told the *New York Times*. (The idea, Barger explained, is to communicate these two big ideas—then drill down within each one, as necessary.) He noted that it's critical to simplify the mission, because "if people on the frontlines don't understand what you're trying to do, forget it. You don't stand a chance of making it work."[6]

- **OXO.** The company, which has become a dominant player in housewares by designing extraordinarily simple and useful gadgets, distilled its mission down to one sentence: "It's about solving problems for every room in the house," according to CEO Alex Lee. The simplicity of that message carries over to everything the company does—which revolves around uncovering some basic, everyday problem a person is having (whether it's peeling potatoes or opening cans of soup) and finding a way to make that task simpler through a tool that looks good, feels good in the hands, and is easy to use. There's nothing fancy or mysterious about anything OXO makes. The company believes, in Lee's words, that "a tea kettle should look like a tea kettle. Not some square box you have to figure out."[7]

- **Google:** Google's guiding principle, "Focus on the user and all else will follow," has helped the company avoid the complexity and clutter that plague so many of its competitors on the Internet. Even as Google continues to expand and add new services, it has maintained a strong and clear connection to customers—as evidenced by the fact that it topped all other companies in Siegel+Gale's 2011 Global Brand Simplicity Index.

The mission statement is only the beginning. Companies that embrace simplification must make sure that all of their communications and processes measure up to the highest standards of clarity. This includes internal communication—which can be just as important as external messaging. Employees can be a brand's most passionate and dedicated advocates, but they must understand and believe in the company's essential message. Too often, what they get from management is jargon and doublespeak. If there is a lack of clarity and honesty in the way you communicate *inside* your company, it can set the tone for how you communicate to outsiders as well. Consistency of tone is critical.

"No man can wear one face to himself and another to the multitude, without finally getting bewildered as to which may be true."

—NATHANIEL HAWTHORNE

Cleveland Clinic provides a good model for how to use clear, consistent internal communication to foster a culture where everyone understands the mission and how to live up to it. The clinic's guiding principle—"patients first"—is used as a mantra by chief executive Toby Cosgrove, who weaves patient experience stories into all of his presentations. Everyone at the hospital, regardless of their job or level, is called a "caregiver." Through this simple vocabulary change, Cleveland Clinic is able send an important signal to everyone throughout the organization about what's expected of them. And the clinic also uses clever mnemonics to help keep all of this clear in employees' minds. For example, it trains its caregivers to always respond to patients with H.E.A.R.T., which stands for: *H*ear the concern, *E*mpathize, *A*pologize, *R*espond with action to the problem, and *T*hank the person for giving you an opportunity to make things right.

The leaders of Cleveland Clinic are cognizant that words only go so far. To foster a culture that embraces certain desired behaviors, you must make it abundantly clear that those behaviors are valued and rewarded. The hospital not only tracks caregivers' interactions with patients; it also displays individual performance ratings and patient satisfaction scores for all to see. During our time at the clinic, it was obvious that the people working there take great pride in their patient satisfaction scores—in fact, it's a fascinating use of data to create a healthy culture of competitiveness, all based around the primary goal of meeting patients' needs.

William D. Green of Accenture confesses that he once sat through a three-day managerial training session at the company and counted "68 things that we told them they needed to do to be successful." As he got up to close the session, Green says, he realized that "it isn't possible for people to remember all this stuff." He then decided that future training advice should focus on three things: competence, confidence, and caring. "When young people are looking for clarity—this is a huge, complex global company, and they wonder how to navigate their way through it—I just tell them that."[8]

> The most complex employee handbook ever? One contender is a JPMorgan Chase booklet "containing 123 principles for staff to follow each day," according to Lucy Kellaway of the *Financial Times*. But also in the running is a Cadbury Schweppes handbook that, according to Kellaway, lays out 144 rules for its managers to "live and breathe."[9]

The need to simplify communications inside the company extends to everything from concise PowerPoint presentations—Zurich Financial Services' James J. Schiro advises sticking to "three slides, three points"—to streamlined memos and documents.[10] Speaking of which, we recommend at the start of any simplification task to create a short document that sets forth the basic principles, objectives, and measures of success. And don't subject that document—or any other piece of communication the company produces—to endless futzing by department managers or company lawyers. A clear, simple draft can easily degenerate when subject matter experts are given too many rounds of revisions. As one of our longtime colleagues, Thia Reggio, says, "Invariably the third round of revisions brings you back to the original, complicated mess." So we recommend this simple rule: *Limit rounds of revisions to two.*

Why complexity thrives among silos

Simplifying a company and its culture goes beyond communication challenges. It can require significant restructuring aimed toward streamlining processes, rooting out layers, and knocking down walls. One major problem is that companies are often divided into vertical silos—a structure that fosters complexity. Each division has its own rules, its own objectives, and its own turf to protect. Meanwhile, the larger, overarching goal—of, say, creating the best overall experience for a customer—becomes splintered and fragmented among specialized, often competing groups within the company.

When Cleveland Clinic transitioned to its "patients first" approach, the leaders took a hard look at how the organization was structured—with an old hierarchy of doctor-based departments. That structure may have made sense for the doctors, but not the patients. So in 2008, Cleveland Clinic reorganized into twenty-three patient-based institutes, combining "rival" disciplines of medicine and surgery under a single leadership for seamless patient care. This meant that if you suffered from a particular condition, you could get everything you needed to deal with that (including equipment, therapists, and so forth) in one location. The structure contributed to a simpler, holistic experience.

Rigid, compartmentalized corporate structures just aren't conducive to creating simple customer experiences, for a number of reasons. As IBM's complexity study found, "Customer insights get lost in silos"; one department may know something important about customers and their needs, but it doesn't necessarily share that with other departments—particularly if no one is taking responsibility for simplifying the overall customer experience. Again, this is where leadership comes in: Simplification must be championed within a company by someone with the authority to cross the silos and unify efforts around a common objective.

Richard Whitehall of Smart Design says this is a major issue in the product design world. Often companies are structured so that one part of the company works on one aspect of the offering. Within these silos, people focus on their individual product line or the component they produce. But as we've moved to more of an "experience economy," Whitehall notes, this approach doesn't work as well; you can segment a product into parts, but a customer experience should be integrated and cohesive. That's why, he says, "In terms of designing the overall experience, you must bring the people charged with different tasks together in project-based teams—so they can all work together on how people will experience this product or service. It's about getting the company to think as a 'whole brain.'"

By taking this more holistic approach to design and product development, you can "bake in" simplicity early in the process. It's a bit like preventive medicine: If you address issues of customer needs in an integrated, holistic manner early on, you can avoid having to cure complexity problems at later stages.

If simplification requires breaking down walls within the company, it also necessitates removing barriers that separate the company from the outside world. We talked about the importance of empathy in enabling companies to simplify. But for companies to be empathetic, the company culture should be one that encourages learning, listening, and engaging directly with the customer. Many businesses (and particularly at the upper executive levels of companies) are not set up for this kind of interaction.

At Cleveland Clinic, the efforts to improve patient experience are based around the idea that the more you engage with patients—and not just superficially, but in a manner that tries to get at their real problems, concerns, and needs—the better you'll be able to serve them. The clinic first began to see the value of this when it increased the amount of "rounding" by nurses—it turned out the more face-to-face contact nurses and patients had, the better for all parties. The success of the nursing rounds has led to "leadership rounding," where the hospital CEO and other top executives tour the units and engage directly with both caregivers and patients.

Simplicity seems to thrive in an open culture, where people are able to communicate more freely—both with insiders and with those outside the company. At OXO, the openness of the culture is apparent as soon as you set foot in its New York head-quarters. Everyone works in a large, open space, with no clear delineation between departments. Multidisciplinary teams work on projects in clusters, but the sketches and prototypes are usually in full view—and anyone can jump in with ideas on any project. Communication within the company tends to be direct, simple, and informal: "Too often in companies, people who work in the same office email each other," says OXO's CEO, Alex Lee.[11]

Most of the people at OXO actually use the kinds of products they work on, so they're able to bring the practical experience of a customer to their work. For example, many of OXO's employees have young children—and they've led the company's recent efforts to design simpler, more practical products for toddlers. Knowing how quickly young children outgrow things, OXO has started designing products such as high chairs that can be converted into chairs for older kids.

But the company doesn't just rely on the expertise that resides within its walls. OXO is unusual in the way it welcomes ideas from outside inventors and designers. (And if you do submit an idea to the company, you won't be buried in legal paperwork, because OXO has taken pains to streamline agreements and simplify its working arrangements with outsiders.)

For example, one idea that came from outside was for a new type of measuring cup designed to be easier to use (see Figure 6.1). *Easier to use? A measuring cup is pretty simple to start with, no?* But the company was intrigued by this idea, and proceeded to do the kind of in-depth empathic research OXO has become known for. According to Lee, OXO sent some of its designers into people's kitchens and watched as those people used standard measuring cups. And they noticed something interesting: Because the typical measuring cup has its levels marked on the side, it forces the user to constantly bend in order to see the measurements.

It was a user problem that no one talked about, the kind of thing that would never surface in focus group research—only by going into people's kitchens and paying attention was OXO able to see that yes, there really was a need for a measuring cup

Figure 6.1

with level markings that could be seen from *above*. The OXO measuring cup sold a couple of million units in its first year, a half of the market.

The value of naïveté

The lesson for OXO was that even though its designers may be experts on kitchen gadgets, there is always room to learn from outsiders. This is why we believe an important principle of simplification is: *Value naïveté.*

There's a good reason for this: Familiarity with a particular area or domain leads to a particular kind of myopia that diminishes the ability to see creeping complexity. It also can give you a deaf ear when it comes to detecting jargon. People who are not insiders or subject experts can bring a fresh set of eyes and ears. Most importantly, they provide a perspective that is closer to that of the customer.

When Philips was starting its corporate simplification initiative, the company recognized that outside inspiration would be essential. It formed a Simplicity Advisory Board with five members from several different industries and professions, including a European fashion designer, an Asian architect, an American radiologist, a professor from MIT, and an automotive designer. The board served as a critical think tank and sounding board for Philips as it tried to rethink its products and policies from a fresh perspective.

Another simplicity master we admire is the software company Intuit. It's common knowledge that Quicken, Intuit's flagship product, was inspired by the company founder's realization that his wife couldn't print her checks. The company was based on the idea of figuring out how nonexperts can be empowered by software to take on specialized business tasks normally handled by experts. This focus on customer-driven simplicity helped Intuit dominate the market with Quicken and TurboTax.

As with many companies devoted to simplicity in product design, the ripple effect in the organization is far-reaching. Like Philips, Intuit is now changing its recruiting process to be shorter and simpler, and it has adopted the same measurement of customer loyalty—the Net Promoter scorecard. Clearly, the methodology of asking just one question as the yardstick for external success has appeal for companies that truly believe in simplicity.

Intuit has adopted a number of processes to keep the company more open and in touch with the reality of users' needs:

- **Site visits and usability lab testing.** Twenty-five hundred people come into their usability labs each year, and they visit fifteen hundred customers at work in the field.
- **Customer councils.** Product development teams form customer councils as needed, with customers typically serving on a council for a year at a time.

- **QuickBooks Challenge.** Company executives pretend that they are customers and call with questions to test the call center.

The company has always valued the input of naïve outsiders. Employees proudly recount the story of the original novice user group formed twenty years ago—a bevy of small-town women nicknamed the "Atherton Dames." Now, when interviewed, company executives shy away from characterizing any one group as particularly naïve, but the notion of finding nonexperts to test their products is very much alive. Intuit also hired an editor from the *Motley Fool* website to write the wording of the TurboTax interface so that it would sound more like a person and less like the tax code.

You don't necessarily have to go outside the company to get a fresh perspective—sometimes it's just a matter of taking a more cross-disciplinary approach by seeking viewpoints from outside the particular department in charge of a project. Going outside the department becomes even more important when the department is Legal—because simplification is almost impossible to achieve if lawyers are calling the shots. For companies to simplify, they must empower the right people, not those who contributed to the complexity in the first place. In fact, it may be necessary to wrest control from those who are inclined to foster complexity. And when we talk about people prone to complicating things, we refer to Exhibit A: company lawyers.

Obviously, companies need lawyers—just not as much as they think they do. Because so many business leaders are risk-averse and perceive their biggest risk to be lawsuits, they elevate lawyers to a position of unchallenged authority, meaning the legal department has the last word. And lawyers, for the most part, have an aversion to simplicity.

For example, lawyers often contend that simplified language is not sufficiently precise; many argue that legislation and court decisions have given precise meanings to the most arcane terms used in consumer contracts so that they will stand up in court. As a practical matter, the legal profession's case for exacting language that will "stand up in court" rests on increasingly shaky ground. Judges in many states are applying the doctrine of *reasonable expectations*, meaning that if you screw your customers, all the boilerplate language in the world may not protect you anyway.

Companies that simplify find ways to keep the legal department in check. One of the secrets of Chubb Insurance's success with their super-simple Masterpiece policy (featured in chapter 2) was that the company didn't let lawyers draft text changes. Instead, a nonlawyer does the drafting, and then lawyers review it for accuracy and compliance. Andrew McElwee Jr., COO of Chubb Personal Insurance (himself a lawyer), marvels at the policy's enduring clarity. He makes the point that "legalese ensures precision" but "Chubb is able to live with a measure of ambiguity because the Chubb business model is not one of nickel and diming customers."

It doesn't hurt to bring in-house lawyers down a peg. ING Direct CEO Arkadi Kuhlmann believes that using humor to show corporate lawyers the extremity of their ways can be quite powerful. By lampooning three-hundred-word footnotes he put the company on the side of the consumer—a sharp contrast to the general perception that banks are out to hoodwink the public.

Hey, New York City: simplify this!

When it comes to overly complex organizations, nothing beats government. And we believe government simplification requires many of the same actions and conditions needed to simplify business: strong leadership, clarity of purpose, and a culture of simplicity that prizes openness, empathy, and innovation.

While it might seem that government is too big and unwieldy to be transformed in this way, we've come upon at least one example that gives us hope. In New York City, Mayor Michael Bloomberg has demonstrated that it's possible to radically simplify the way one of the largest cities in the world communicates with its residents. New York's 311 telephone system handles fifteen million calls per year, covering a wide range of complaints, inquiries, and mini-crises—everything from leaking fire hydrants to gaping potholes.[12]

The program was born out of empathy: Bloomberg's administration asked New Yorkers what problems they were having with city services and learned that people had difficulty accessing those services—there were too many departments, too many numbers to call. The challenge was to change the perception of city government from bureaucratic, fragmented, and officious to approachable and simple.

Bloomberg announced that he was going to simplify the system within one year. (It actually took fourteen months, but hey, that's close enough—and it confirms our belief that even ambitious simplification programs can and should be rolled out quickly.) Bloomberg was the driving force, but since technology was critical to the solution, he tapped Gino Menchini, commissioner of the city's Department of Information Technology and Telecommunications, to achieve this "customer service facelift."

Talk about "distilling": Ultimately, Menchini's team would replace fourteen pages of listings in the city directory—thousands of phone numbers—with one phone number, 311. In the process, he consolidated forty call centers into two.

When we visited the 311 call center, we could see right away that the focus was on customer service—which (sad to say) is not what one generally expects to find at a government-run operation. In plain view to all in the center is an electronic "tote" board that changes from green to yellow to red to indicate call delays or spikes in volume. Unlike a corporate call center, where call takers are often measured on how quickly they can end a call, these representatives are rated on the accuracy of the information they provide and the successful resolution of the caller's problem (see Figure 6.2).

To make the system work, each city department cataloged

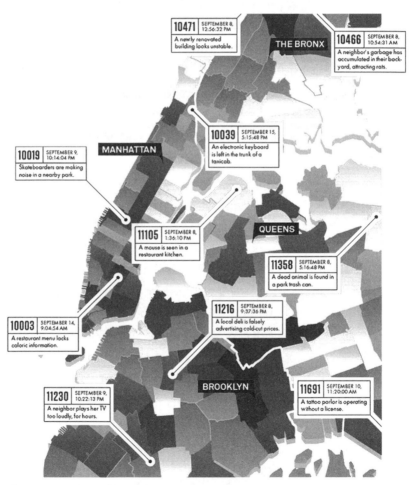

Figure 6.2

and tagged its subject matter to create a giant content library accessed by keyword searches (much like popular Internet search engines use). Part of the system's usefulness lies in its constant refinement of the search engine based upon how frequently each topic arises.

The "citizen service representatives" who answer the incoming calls are specially trained to pick out the pertinent phrases from callers' often disjointed complaints or explanations. Representatives undergo four-week "probing questions" training to help them quickly determine what the problem is, and the call takers' computer screens are remarkably user-friendly, with clearly labeled buttons titled "What," "Where," "Who," "Next Steps," and "How Resolved."

The beauty of the 311 operation is that it hides the complexity of city bureaucracy from the public. Of course, all of those legacy systems and departments of a big city are still there—but people calling 311 don't have to deal with them. Instead, it's up to the trained call takers to figure out how to resolve the problem or, if necessary, smoothly transfer the caller to a legacy system within the 311 call center.

Simplification sometimes has unanticipated benefits, and in the case of 311 one of the pleasant surprises is that it has turned out to be a great learning tool for the city. Each complaint is logged, tagged, and mapped—so it helps the city's leaders to get outside the bubble and understand the real needs of New Yorkers, while also seeing which areas of the city may be experiencing particular problems. For example, seeing a pattern of noise complaints in certain areas led to a series of noise abatement programs. The 311 system also shows the amount of time it takes agencies to resolve issues, which reveals whether the various city departments and agencies are performing well. The system even accepts feedback regarding the mayor's performance, with anonymous comments passed along to Bloomberg's office in the form of a spreadsheet.

By being forced to simplify itself, the city has become aware of policies and procedures that were overly complex for no good reason. As Menchini said to us, "The 311 project served as a catalyst to change the city's procedures, not just explain them." He cites the ever popular "tree blocking sign" call as a classic example. Previously, when a person called in to report a tree blocking a sign, they might have had to deal with either the Parks Department or the Department of Transportation—believe it or not, it depended upon which part of the tree (branch or trunk) was blocking the sign! Thankfully, the city has now changed its procedures so that one department handles all such complaints.

Following on the success of 311, the simplicity warrior Bloomberg has taken aim at other New York complexities and bureaucracies. For example, a new program has been set up to help start-up restaurants in the city cut through red tape. The two-year-old New Business Acceleration Team expedites the process of getting restaurant permits and approvals from the various municipal departments—which results in new restaurants being able to open their doors seventy-two days sooner, on average. That's good news for business owners and hungry diners, but it also is putting millions of dollars in additional tax revenues in the city's coffers.[13]

As for the 311 program, it has taken more than one hundred million calls—and even though they come in at a rate of fifty thousand a day, most callers are connected to a live rep within thirty seconds. Perhaps the most remarkable aspect of the program is that it has given New Yorkers a voice in helping to address the city's everyday problems and snafus—and there's always someone there on the line to listen and respond. As *Wired* magazine observed, "311 is designed to re-create some of the human touch of small-town life in the context of a vast metropolis."[14]

If you can bring a small-town touch to New York, you can simplify any complex organization. But there are a few key points to keep in mind. Strategic simplification must be tackled in broad sweeping strokes. If you merely address isolated areas, or try to simplify via baby steps and incremental change, it's too easy to lose momentum. The metrics for evaluation will be too insignificant; executive focus will wane; too few customers will see the impact; and you'll lose any dramatic sense of change. And drama is important: It can help capture the hearts and loyalties of customers, while rallying people inside the company around something that feels like an actual transformation.

Yet even if the simplification initiative is bold and broad in scope, you won't vanquish complexity overnight. Indeed, you can't kill complexity: The best you can do is move it away from your customers, keep it out of sight as much as possible, and remain vigilant—because it's likely to come creeping back. This is why it's better to think of simplification as a journey, not a destination.

- - - - - - - - - - - - - - - - - - - -

CHAPTER 7

Where Do We Go from Here?

Social Media Empowers Simplifiers

THE SIMPLICITY MOVEMENT WON'T BE LED BY
THOSE WHO FOSTERED COMPLEXITY IN THE FIRST
PLACE. IT'S UP TO THE REST OF US TO DEMAND
CLARITY FROM COMPANIES AND GOVERNMENT
AND INSTILL THOSE VALUES IN OUR DAILY LIVES.
HERE'S HOW TO BECOME A "SIMPLICITY WARRIOR."

We've been invested in the mission of simplification for more than three decades. During that time, we've seen interest in this cause rise and subside. We've had many people tell us they think it's important and worthwhile to fight for simplicity. But few have had the motivation or the gumption to join us in tackling this challenge head-on. They may have sensed

> *"A little simplification would be the first step toward rational living, I think."*
> —ELEANOR ROOSEVELT

that there was a potential opportunity for them, but it wasn't mission-critical.

Something has changed recently, however. People have begun to fight as never before for clarity, transparency, and fairness in their dealings with business and government. More and more are becoming simplicity warriors—without the need for a Nader-like leader. They're doing it themselves, armed only with social media and a healthy sense of outrage.

Case in point: 2011's grassroots uprising against banks' attempt to levy new fees on customers (such as a $5 monthly debit card fee). People noticed it, and more importantly, they began to talk about it (and blog about it, and tweet about it). One person, twenty-two-year-old Molly Katchpole of Washington, D.C., created an online petition to scrap the fee. Within a month, she had rounded up three hundred thousand signatures. The groundswell was too much for banks to ignore. A little over a month after the planned fee was announced, the banks reversed themselves.[1]

In the fall of the same year, not long after Katchpole had begun circulating her online petition, a Los Angeles art gallery owner named Kristen Christian began organizing an event called "Bank Transfer Day." Using Facebook and other forms of social media, Christian proposed that frustrated customers teach the major banks a lesson by withdrawing accounts en masse in the first week of November and transferring the money to smaller, not-for-profit credit unions. Nearly a hundred thousand people on Facebook responded favorably to the idea right away; by the time Bank Transfer Day actually arrived, 650,000 people had moved from large banks to credit unions in just one month.[2]

These were just two of many instances in which people used the newfound power of social media to band together against an unpopular corporate decision or policy, a seemingly unfair provision in a contract, or a perceived attempt to "put one over" on the public. While the disappearance of brick-and-mortar stores has made companies seem more ephemeral, their proximity is actually just a click away—and most importantly, each consumer is now part of a community of shoppers who would previously have been invisible to each other. By squawking online through tweets, blogs, Facebook postings, and so on, we make our confusion, displeasure, or praise known instantaneously.

This single change is the reason why the clamor for simplicity will reach a fever pitch over the next few years, and that will be for the good of commerce and government. We're witnessing the formation of a completely new power base that simply didn't exist at the time of earlier consumer movements. This grassroots base has numbers on its side and the capacity to bring about change and reform in ways that earlier movements could not.

Movements are often fueled by anger, and the burgeoning simplicity movement is no exception. People are fed up. Recent surveys show that a majority of people blame complexity for the economic crisis, and rightly so—consumers have begun to realize that some companies deliberately foster confusion to keep us in the dark. The erosion of trust is accompanied by an uneasy sense that our established systems and institutions (from the tax code to Medicare to the financial system) aren't working anymore, in large part because they're drowning in their own complexity.

That people are conducting more of their business online has added a whole new layer of complexity, as exemplified by the growing outcry over click-through agreements. Every minute of every day, people are giving away their rights with the click of a mouse—and you're probably one of them.

Don't laugh: You may not realize it, but click enough times on online user agreements and other virtual contracts, as we all do today, and you'll end up beholden to companies in ways you'd never imagine. Our colleague Leanne Libert pointed out that "sometimes all you have to do is look at something online and you've consented to an agreement."

Libert recently wondered, How many agreements am I a party to? So she proceeded to spend about ninety minutes hunting down many of the click-through agreements and terms of service she'd previously accepted. Her search turned up fifty-three agreements, totaling almost four hundred pages. "It took me ninety minutes to find those documents," she says, "but it would take ninety days to read and digest the information in them."

She did discover, from a little dig into the documents, that she now has legally binding relationships with thirty-four entities, from banks and health insurance companies to shopping websites. "That's right, I'm legally entangled in some of the largest corporations of our time." Libert points out, "If something goes awry under one of these agreements, who do you think will come out on top?"

Not Libert, that's for sure: About half of the agreements she "signed" include "pre-dispute arbitration clauses." Translation: "I gave up my right to sue the other party in court," Libert explains. "How are we supposed to feel about giving up our rights without even knowing it?"

There's another approach, used by the site Bagcheck.com. They divide the terms of use page into two columns. On the left you get the full mess of legalese, and on the right, the "Plain English Highlights" (see Figure 7.1).

We're seeing progress on a number of fronts. The Pew Charitable Trusts is a great example of a nonprofit foundation taking the lead in developing new simplification models that could benefit bank customers. Pew's research showed that the median length of bank disclosures for key checking policies and fee information was 111 pages. Responding to this, Pew developed a model disclosure form—similar to a nutrition label for food—to provide consumers with clear information about fees, terms, and conditions of their checking accounts.

Figure 7.2 shows what the Pew Model Disclosure Box looks like.

Simple

Bagcheck   HOME   ABOUT   JOIN   SIGN IN   [   ]

TERMS | PRIVACY | COPYRIGHT

Terms of Use

Here are the laws of our land with a translation from their original Legalese for your reading pleasure.

Terms of Use	Plain English Highlights
Bagcheck Inc. ("Bagcheck", "we", "us", or "our") provides the website located at www.bagcheck.com, including the mobile version of the website, (collectively, the "Site"), software we make available through the Site (e.g., widgets) (if any) ("Site Software"), and software we make available for mobile devices (e.g., an iphone or android application) (if any) ("Mobile Software") (collectively, the "Service"). The Service allows users to share perspectives on their favorite products and how they use them.	Plain English Highlights are provided for your convenience only and do not represent a legally binding agreement. Please read the Terms of Use (to the left) to understand the legally binding terms for your use of the service.
These Terms of Use ("Agreement") contain the legally binding terms for your use of the Service. By visiting, accessing or using the Service, you are accepting this Agreement and you represent and warrant that you have the right, authority, and capacity to enter into this Agreement. If you do not agree with all of the provisions of this Agreement, please do not access and/or use the Service.	By using this service, you are agreeing to this Agreement.

1. Accounts

1.1 Account Creation

In order to use certain features of the Service, you must register for an account with Bagcheck ("Account") and provide certain information about yourself as prompted by the Service registration form. You represent and warrant that: (a) all required registration information you submit is truthful and accurate; and (b) you will maintain the accuracy of such information. You may delete your Account at any time, for any reason, by following the instructions on the Service. Bagcheck may suspend or terminate your Account in accordance with Section 8. If we reasonably believe your account name violates the Community Guidelines or otherwise violates this Agreement, we reserve the right to modify or delete your Account name or suspend or terminate your

You have to create an account to use certain features of the service.

You must provide accurate account registration information and keep it accurate.

Bagcheck   © 2011 Bagcheck Inc. | About | Blog | Help | Terms | Got Feedback?

Figure 7.1   Bagcheck.com Terms of Use web page.

Where Do We Go from Here?

HIDDEN RISKS: THE CASE FOR SAFE AND TRANSPARENT CHECKING ACCOUNTS

Pew's Model Disclosure Box for Checking Accounts

BASIC TERMS AND CONDITIONS

Account Opening and Usage	Minimum Deposit Needed to Open Account	$	
	Monthly Fee	$	
	Requirements to Waive Monthly Fee		Minimum combined account balance, direct deposit or other conditions
	Interest Rate	%	
	ATM Fees	$	for using your bank's ATM
	ATM Fees	$	for using another bank's ATM
	Non-Sufficient Funds (NSF) Fee	$	per item
	Returned Check Fee	$	per declined check written to your account
	Stop Payment Fee	$	per item to stop payment for up to X months
	Account Closing Fee	$	if account closed within Y days of opening
	Other Service Fees		Please consult the back of this document for a list of additional service fees.
Overdraft Options for Consumers with Debit Cards	Option A: (Default) — No Overdraft Service		If you choose not to opt in to any kind of overdraft service, transactions that would cause an overdraft will be declined at no cost to you.
	Option B: — Overdraft Transfer Fee	$	per overdraft covered by transfer from linked savings account, line of credit or credit card
	Option C: Overdraft Penalty — Overdraft Penalty Fee	$	per overdraft covered by bank advance
	Maximum Number of Overdraft Penalty Fees per Day		
	Extended Overdraft Penalty Fee	$	every Mth day the account is overdrawn, starting N days after the account is first overdrawn
Processing Policies	Posting Order — The order in which withdrawals and deposits are processed		Summary of policy
	Deposit Hold Policy — When funds deposited to your account are available		• Cash deposit with teller: X business day • Cash deposit at ATM: X business day • Check deposit with teller: Y business day • Check deposit at ATM: Y business day • Direct deposit: X business day • Wire transfer: X business day • If something causes a longer hold on a deposit, the first $200 of that deposit will be made available either the same business day of the deposit or the next business day. • Funds from non-bank checks may take an extra business day to become available. A "business day" is a non-holiday weekday. The end of a business day varies by branch, but it is no earlier than T p.m.
Dispute Resolution	Dispute Resolution Agreement		Summary of agreement

www.pewtrusts.org/safechecking

Figure 7.2

185

Pew is also doing a good job of getting this new model out there into the world, using new media to influence government and business. According to Susan Weinstock, the director of Pew's Safe Checking Project, once the idea for the disclosure box was developed, the foundation put a petition online (at Care2.org) to gather public support behind the initiative. The goal is to get the government, through the Consumer Financial Protection Bureau, to consider adopting this model for banks. That hasn't happened yet, but nevertheless, one bank, Chase, has already agreed to test out the Pew Model in its own dealings with customers.

Speaking of the CFPB, its very formation, in 2011, marked a watershed moment in the current simplicity movement. Buoyed by the early unofficial leadership of consumer advocate Elizabeth Warren and subsequently by the new group's first director, Richard Cordray, the CFPB has initiated a national dialogue (one that has been sorely needed for years) about the rights of consumers and the perils of fine print.

The CFPB has been attempting to bring greater clarity to all manner of personal financial transactions: mortgages, payday lending, student loans, and credit cards. For each of these, the group has created, or is creating, a shortened, simpler form to explain the essence of each type of transaction.

The CFPB's version of a new, simpler credit card agreement is shown in Figure 7.3.

Welcome to ABC Bank.

You'll find the terms of your credit card here.
It's a contract that starts as soon as you sign or use the card.

For each underlined word or phrase, the definition in the Consumer Financial Protection Bureau Definition of Credit Card Terms is part of your contract.

These definitions are available at www.cfpb.gov or www.abcbank.com. Or call 1-800-xxx-xxxx for a free printed copy.

1. Costs

You may use your card for purchases, cash advances, or balance transfers. Each type of charge will have its own balance. Each balance may have a separate interest rate.

What are the charges?

Interest rate for [period] on purchases	X% APR	→ Interest rate after [period] on purchases		X% APR
Interest rate on balance transfers	X% APR	+ Balance transfer fee (per transaction)		X%
Interest rate on cash advances	X% APR	+ Cash advance fee (per transaction)		X%
Penalty interest rate	X% APR	Late payment fee		$X/$Y
Returned payment fee	$X	Rush card fee		$X
Replacement card fee	$X	Foreign currency transaction fee		X%

Your APRs are variable, except [excluded rates]. They increase or decrease with the prime rate. From the [day] of each billing period, we apply APRs based on the prime rate published x business days before the end of that period. To determine your APRs we add to the prime rate: x percentage points for purchases after [period], x percentage points for balance transfers, x percentage points for cash advances, and x percentage points for the penalty interest rate.

What do I have to pay and when?

We will send your bill to the address on file. You agree to pay all authorized charges on the bill, including interest and fees. You agree to pay us for charges that we allow over your credit limits. You must pay at least the minimum payment by the due date stated on each bill. Your minimum payment will be [insert formula].

We choose which balances to pay with the minimum payment. We apply payments above the minimum to balances with the highest APRs first.

You must pay in U.S. dollars, without restrictive terms, and according to all the other standard payment instructions. Mailed payments should be sent to [payment address].

What if I pay late?

If you don't pay at least the minimum payment by the due date, you'll be charged a late payment fee of $X.

In addition, if you make a late payment, you will be in default and you may be subject to interest rate increases.

If you are late more than once in a six month period, the late payment fee will go up to $Y. If you make on time payments for six months, it will return to $X.

Special Promotions

How is interest calculated?

We calculate interest using the daily balance method with compounding. This means that interest compounds daily.

We will not charge you interest on purchases if you pay your full account balance by the due date each month. This is called a grace period. If you do not take advantage of the grace period, we will charge interest starting the day you make a purchase. If you do not pay your full account balance on time in any month you will lose your grace period until you pay your full account balance on time x months in a row. You pay interest on cash advances or balance transfers from [date].

Figure 7.3

*   *   *

All of these attempts to create new models for simplifying our everyday transactions are important first steps—and should be supported and applauded. *We must powerfully exert our influence as consumers and as citizens.* When we see examples, like the ones previously cited, of companies or organizations that *are* striving to provide greater clarity and transparency in their dealings with the public, we should spread the word through social media. We can change buying habits to reward companies that inform rather than obfuscate, remind companies that they hurt themselves when they sacrifice customer loyalty to cut costs, push public institutions to provide transparency, and petition lawmakers and regulators to demand responsibility from those who are abetting the complexity crisis.

As consumers and vocal members of the public, we can call out the companies and public institutions that muddle their messages, complicate their offerings, and conceal their intentions—much the way Deborah Adler challenged the prescription drug industry or Molly Katchpole took on the banks.

Call for clarity

To help foster and support this kind of grassroots activity, we have been building, over the past year, a place that would-be simplicity warriors can call home. Under the banner of "Call for Clarity" (www.callforclarity.com) we've set up a clearinghouse and a shared platform designed to serve the needs of the simplicity movement.

Our goal is to educate and enlighten people on what's going on in the movement—what issues are at stake, who's doing things right and who's in the wrong, and what actions can be taken by you. One of the most important things we can do, of course, is to connect people who share the same interest and passion on this issue. The callforclarity.com site includes a forum where people share their own experiences and stories about waging war against complexity. It's also a place to share strategies—ways of influencing companies and government agencies, techniques for using social media and other tools to spread the word and be heard on this issue.

We've identified several critical areas that require attention and solutions. As a case in point, let's take a look at what's going on with *student loans.* If (like a distracted student) you haven't been paying attention, you might not be aware that this is shaping up as quite possibly the subprime mortgage crisis of 2015. It is *that* serious.

Student debt now totals $800 billion, surpassing the total credit card debt of all Americans.[3] Right now, teenagers are assuming tens of thousands of dollars' worth of debt with little understanding of how it will affect their lives.

So what can be done? For starters, all of America's colleges ought to adopt a simplified, standard financial award letter so parents and students can make comparisons across schools. In those letters, financial award terms should be clustered and ranked in order of value, from free (grants and scholarships) to the most costly. We must make it clear to families that not all aid money is equal—and some will have long strings attached.

It would certainly help for students and parents to have a financial aid "shopping sheet"—like the one that has been suggested by the CFPB, shown in Figure 7.4.

When it comes to student loans, parents are even more confused than their kids. Our survey of parents of college-age children who've applied for financial aid found that 77 percent did not know the difference between a subsidized and an unsubsidized loan, and less than half knew that not all student loans require a credit check.[4]

Part of our challenge in the call for clarity is to find ways to build support—and provide constructive input—on ideas such as this one, while also developing our own model for clear, simplified financial award letters (with input from you, if you have ideas). But the idea, beyond that, is to set up a clearinghouse of information on this subject: to let students and parents know about tools that may be available to them; to inform them about who the key players are to be contacted (that is, pressured) on this issue. We'll share that information, and vari-

University of the United States (UUS)
Private 4-year

Example only,
fictional data

How to pay for college   Prepared for Abigail Adams, first year student

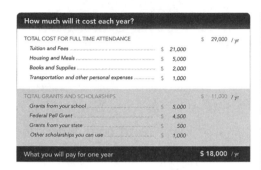

How much will it cost each year?

TOTAL COST FOR FULL TIME ATTENDANCE		$ 29,000 / yr
Tuition and Fees	$ 21,000	
Housing and Meals	$ 5,000	
Books and Supplies	$ 2,000	
Transportation and other personal expenses	$ 1,000	
TOTAL GRANTS AND SCHOLARSHIPS		$ 11,000 / yr
Grants from your school	$ 5,000	
Federal Pell Grant	$ 4,500	
Grants from your state	$ 500	
Other scholarships you can use	$ 1,000	
What you will pay for one year		**$ 18,000** / yr

What are your loan and work study options?

FEDERAL LOANS THAT YOU ARE ELIGIBLE FOR		$ 8,000 / yr
Perkins Loan	$ 2,500	
Subsidized Stafford Loan	$ 3,000	
Unsubsidized Stafford Loan	$ 2,500	
FEDERAL WORK STUDY		$ 4,000 / yr
PRIVATE STUDENT LOANS		$ 6,000 / yr

After graduation, how much will you owe?

ESTIMATED MONTHLY PAYMENT FOR FEDERAL LOANS		$ 411 / mth
Estimated total federal loan debt	$ 37,000	
ESTIMATED MONTHLY PAYMENT FOR PRIVATE LOANS		$ 297 / mth
Estimated total private loan debt	$ 26,000	
YOUR TOTAL ESTIMATED DEBT	$ 63,000	
Your estimated monthly payment for all loans		**$ 708** / mth

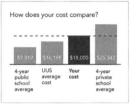

How does your cost compare?

$9,819	$16,198	$18,000	$25,343
4-year public school average	UUS average cost	Your cost	4-year private school average

UUS student loan default rate

The percentage of students from this school who defaulted on their Federal Stafford loans within the first 3 years of repayment.

6.2%

| LOW | MEDIUM | HIGH |

UUS graduation rates

The percentage of students who graduate within 6 years

71%	75%
UUS average	4-year private school average

UUS retention rates

The percentage of non-graduating students who re-enroll the following year

72%	80%
UUS average	4-year private school average

University of the United States (UUS)

Financial Aid Office
123 Main Street
Anytown, ST 12345

(123) 456-7890
financialaid@uus.edu

For further explanation and next steps, visit **http://www.url.com/school/personalurl**

Figure 7.4

ous other strategies, with you—and together we just might be able to head off this crisis before it's too late.

Student loans is just one issue we're focused on. Among the others:

- Simplifying the **tax code** (by way of a progressive flat tax).
- Continuing to develop models for simplified **credit card agreements** (while also applying pressure on government agencies and credit card companies to actually adopt the new models).
- Working to bring more clarity and transparency to online **click-through agreements.**
- Developing and pushing for simpler **insurance policies.**
- Calling for **clearer hospital bills** and **patient discharge instructions.**
- Bringing clarity to **auto leases** and **car loans.**
- Working to simplify and bring transparency to **mortgages** (hopefully before the next meltdown).
- Simplifying **jury instructions** (if you've served on a jury, you know what we're talking about).

These are some of the issues where the need for simplification is most pressing. But in general terms, we can expect the crisis of complexity to affect our lives more deeply, and in more ways, in the coming years. One reason is our aging population; while all of us crave simplicity, this growing segment has a critical need for clarity in the face of complex technology and a mounting onslaught of information. Indeed, we're all likely to be drowning in data as the demand for greater transparency and disclosure provides us with all the information we're asking for—and much, much more. It will be more critical than ever, in the days ahead, to demand *real transparency* in the information provided to us. So while we support calls for greater disclosure by companies or government agencies, we must remember that none of this will help unless we insist that the information disclosed is relevant, streamlined, well organized, designed and visualized for greater clarity, supported by relevant examples, and written in plain language.

Meanwhile, all of us will need to be on the lookout for what we call **faux simplicity**—a term we coined to describe the current epidemic of marketers claiming to be champions or purveyors of simplicity when in fact they're anything but. It's no wonder companies are trying to co-opt simplicity; they've begun to realize that consumers will seek out and even be willing to pay a premium for it. These marketers are smart enough to figure this out. They're just not willing to figure out how to deliver the real thing. They don't care to empathize; they can't be bothered to distill; they don't know how to clarify. But knowing that the mere mention of the word "simple" is a hook for purchasers, advertisers and marketers now stock their copy with the words "easy," "convenient," "quick," and "simplified." However, slapping the label "simple" on something that looks like the instruction manual for the space shuttle will surely backfire when purchasers feel betrayed. Practicing faux simplicity is even worse than being just plain complicated. Dante viewed opportunists as minor sinners, dwelling on the outskirts of hell to be perpetually plagued by wasps, hornets, and, we presume, their consciences. As simplifiers, we view opportunists who use simplicity as a come-on even more harshly. We recommend they stock up on calamine lotion.

It's up to consumers to police these companies—to call them out when they try to mislead their customers. But there's also a role for business to self-police and to be more vocal in championing simplicity. We're bringing big business directly into the discussion by inviting CEOs to take part. At the same time, there's a critical role in this movement for consumer watchdog groups, large foundations (listen up, Pew, Gates, and MacArthur Foundations), nonprofits, and political leaders to get involved and actively support the cause. Educators are a major part of this initiative as well—in particular, professors at business schools, law schools, and medical schools must address this issue, because when it comes to the proliferation of jargon, the professional schools are ground zero.

The most important partner we must enlist in this cause is you. We want to tap into your ideas, your social networks, your passion to bring about change. At the same time, we're trying to make it easier for you to take advantage of the many available resources that can help anyone take positive action in the battle against complexity. Today there are apps that can help you bypass those phone trees that waste your time and keep you from getting real answers from actual human beings; there are organizations, such as the Center for Plain Language, where you can learn more about ongoing efforts to deal with the escalation of jargon; there are watchdog sites where you can submit particularly egregious examples of misleading fine print; there are consumer activist resources—such as Consumerist.com or (and you've got to love this name) PissedConsumer.com—designed to help you take action against companies that fail to provide what's expected and deserved. The resources are many and they're out there, but until now they haven't been consolidated in one place. At www.callforclarity.com, we've brought them together and explained what each can do for you and how to best use them.

Ultimately, the simplicity movement will be led by those of us who've been on the receiving end of too much confusion for too long. One of the great misconceptions about the complexity crisis is the belief that the people who made things so complicated—the bureaucrats, the technocrats, the lawyers—are the only ones who can get us out of this mess. But if we wait for help from those who've developed and fostered the confusion, we may be waiting a long time.

It's time for us to demand—or, if in leadership positions, to develop and put into effect—new ways of borrowing money, of paying taxes, of accessing government services, of purchasing products, of communicating.

- **We can transform the way we do business.** Those of us in the business realm have the power and the opportunity to apply principles of simplicity to all aspects of business, and in so doing to strengthen our businesses while improving consumer experiences.
- **We can reinvent the everyday practices and processes plagued by complexity.** Everything from paying our taxes to voting to getting a mortgage—these processes and dozens of others need to be rethought with a focus on simplification, streamlining, and clarification.

The simplicity movement spawned in the 1970s lacked the magic bullet we have today—social media. Our technological grapevine provides the ability to share our frustrations instantaneously and effect societal change. In the section that follows, you'll find a wealth of resources to help you get started—and you'll find even more at the www.callforclarity .com site. There are lots of ways to become a part-time or full-fledged simplicity warrior, including ways to link yourself to the larger movement, get your business involved, your community, your local politicians. You can pressure organizations to simplify, push for government regulation that demands simplification, demand transparency and plain English policies in all public programs, and take on the enemies of simplicity. We're not saying it'll be easy or instantaneous, but hopefully, in the end, it will be *simple.*

As We Go to Press

It is now December 2012, and this book is about to be put to bed. Timing is everything in life, and much to our pleasure and excitement, simplicity is in the news as never before. Just this week, a survey conducted by Common Good—the nonpartisan government reform coalition we mentioned earlier in this book, headed by Philip K. Howard—sponsored a telephone survey conducted by Clarus Research Group with a sample of 1,000 registered voters nationwide. The key findings were that 85 percent of respondents favored simplifying government rules and regulations, 93 percent think that Congress and the president should overhaul government programs with the goal of eliminating those that duplicate functions, and 81 percent think that making regulations "simpler and less complex" would help the economy create jobs.

Since most people really have very little knowledge of how many government regulations there are or what they cover, we believe that people are basically expressing impatience and lack of confidence in government bureaucracy. They are weary of endless arguments and debates on the part of politicians who recount hard-to-follow statistics, recite acronyms, and speak in jargon. People are overwhelmed by quantity and complexity and are seeking a "back to basics" approach as a way to regain comprehension and control.

The results of the Common Good survey crossed paths with a December 9, 2012, opinion piece by Daniel Akst in the *New York Times Sunday Review,* titled "Those Crazy Indemnity Forms We All Sign." Focusing on the lopsided balance of power represented by releases that we are asked to sign to participate in the activities of daily life, from playing sports to selling online, he called on people to start objecting rather than merely griping. More than a hundred people added their online comments in response to his article describing their personal experiences not only with indemnity clauses but also with other provisions of legal agreements and contracts that they felt were unrealistically onerous or unenforceable.

Reading the survey and the opinion piece in rapid succession just reinforces our belief that the perennial existence of these unintelligible, unenforceable provisions would come to an end if they were expressed in plain English. It is only because consumers do not understand the meaning of many provisions that the clauses continue to be included on a routine basis. If they clearly understood the imbalance of power, the injustice of the provisions, and the impracticality of the clauses, they wouldn't meekly sign. They would challenge companies by striking out offensive clauses, blogging on the Web to increase awareness, and taking their business elsewhere.

Several recent books give us hope that the uprising has begun and demonstrate just how many different dimensions there are to the topic of simplicity. Duane Elgin's 1981 book, *Voluntary Simplicity*, rereleased in 2010, is about living with balance as a way to achieve happiness. In fact, "How can I simplify my life?" is the question that we get asked the most when people realize what we do for a living. The drive to remove noise and clutter in our daily lives is a common quest, because coping with information overload demands so much time and concentration that it is exhausting and psychologically depleting.

Other recent books cover the topic of simplicity as well. Margaret Jane Radin, a law professor at the University of Michigan, explores intimidating contracts in her book *Boilerplate: The Fine Print, Vanishing Rights, and the Rule of Law. Insanely Simple* by Ken Segall, released in 2012, explores Apple's focus on simplicity as a point of competitive differentiation.

We believe that the time has come in the "me too" world of business when companies will realize that the pursuit of simplicity is a process that will not only streamline their production but also sharpen their focus, empower their employees, reinforce their customer relationships, and increase their profits. It will become unacceptable for employees to add mind-numbing legal provisions as they sit around conference tables. Instead, rewards will be showered upon those who dare to dream up simpler, more meaningful customer experiences rather than tweak archaic legacy provisions.

The recent flurry of books and blog posts about simplicity, coupled with the consumer backlash against complexity, point to a basic desire to understand our legal obligations, our investments, our rights as citizens, and our healthcare options. Consumer confidence can only be born from comprehension, and simplicity offers a greater chance of comprehension. As consumers grow more confident they will spend more, and both our economy and our society will benefit.

We are feeling a groundswell now, and by the time this book is published in 2013, we anticipate even greater consumer clamor for simplicity, more books to be written about the benefits of clarity, and empathetic responses from companies.

RESOURCES

Also available in interactive form on the website
www.callforclarity.com

For Consumers

As we've mentioned, there are two sides to the equation. If
you're on the business side, you can use the case studies and
principles in this book to reevaluate your current business
practices. But even if you're not in the C-suite, you can effect
change as a consumer. We've collected some resources and
tools to help you take control and demand simplicity where it's
absent. First, know your rights. Second, make more informed
decisions. Third, demand what you deserve. Fourth, call out
companies with complaints. Fifth, support simple start-ups.

1. **Know Your Rights**
   - Federal Trade Commission, "Consumer Information"
     http://www.ftc.gov/bcp/consumer.shtm

   As the FTC website says, "education is the first line of
   defense...make well-informed decisions before you
   spend your money." The FTC lays out in certain terms

what your rights are as a consumer and how to make smart decisions in different business sectors. You can order their print publications or explore online.

- USA.gov, "Consumer Protection"
  http://www.usa.gov/topics/consumer.shtml

USA.gov publishes a free Consumer Action Handbook, but we know you may not have the time or inclination to order it, read it, and then take action. Action is best taken when steam is still bursting from your ears! So if that's the case, visit one of the complaint sites that follow.

2. Make More Informed Decisions

- BBC, *Watchdog*
  http://www.bbc.co.uk/watchdog

For a bit of enriching entertainment, BBC One's show *Watchdog* discusses corporate behavior, calls out crooked practices, and offers consumer advice.

- *Virtual Gumshoe*
  http://www.virtualgumshoe.com

Access a free consumer directory and credit reports.

- *Consumer World*
  http://www.consumerworld.org

Consumer World encourages awareness, provides consumer resources, and advises you on smart purchases.

- *The Consumerist*
  http://www.consumerist.com

The Consumerist is a great website for getting the lay of the land—who's naughty, who's nice, who's honest, who's not. Articles are written with wit and candor, so it can simultaneously be a fun and educational read. The Consumerist also has a great collection of how-to articles based on how much you want to get done if a company has given you the short end of the stick.

- *PULSE of NY*
  http://www.pulseofny.org

PULSE is a nonprofit organization dedicated to increasing patient safety through training courses and advocacy. By teaching family members how to navigate the healthcare system and demand knowledge from practitioners, the safety of a patient isn't hinged on his/her own presence of mind, which often suffers under the fear and confusion that health problems and white coats can raise.

- *PBS Kids*, "Don't Buy It"
  http://www.pbskids.org/dontbuyit

It's never too early to start learning how to be a smart consumer in today's global economy. This PBS website instructs kids on how and when to make smart decisions.

FOR CHUCKLES

- *Complaints Choirs Worldwide*
  http://www.complaintschoir.org/choirs.html
- *Lowering the Bar*
  http://www.loweringthebar.net

3. Demand What You Deserve

Telling someone to "go climb a tree" is a fast way to burn bridges. Unfortunately, hundreds of companies tell their customers to go climb a phone tree every day. These sites help you speak with a human or at least get the automated services to leave you alone.

- *FastCustomer*
  http://www.fastcustomer.com

This website saves you the time and frustration of being on hold or struggling through an automated customer service line. Simply tell FastCustomer who you want to talk to and then they'll get that service rep to call "ASAP." You can go online, text, call, or use one of their apps for help anywhere and any time.

- *Gethuman*
  http://www.gethuman.com

This website lets you search for customer service numbers by company or department, rather than calling the general number and then getting transferred and transferred... and transferred until you're finally talking to someone who can help you. Like FastCustomer, you can also get many of the 8,000 listed companies to call you.

- *800notes*
  http://www.800notes.com

Get those pesky 800s to just stop calling.

4. Call Out Companies with Complaints

READ THESE ARTICLES TO MAKE YOUR COMPLAINTS COUNT:

- David Segal, "A Guide to Complaints That Get Results," *New York Times*, May 22, 2010
  http://www.nytimes.com/2010/05/23/your-money/23haggler.html

- Chris Morran, "The Dos and Don'ts of Getting Someone to Take Your Complaint Seriously," The Consumerist, November 2, 2012 http://consumerist.com/2012/11/02/the-dos-and -donts-of-getting-someone-to-take-your -complaint-seriously

VISIT THESE SITES TO GET COMPLAINING:

- Planet Feedback
  http://www.planetfeedback.com

This is a site for some constructive criticism. Sometimes a cathartic venting in letter form is exactly what the doctor ordered. Here, you can write a letter to a company explaining your grievances. And the best part? Some companies monitor the site and will respond to your letter! We provide some sites for venting, some for exposing, but this one seems to be the best for starting a conversation.

- Ripoff Report
  http://www.ripoffreport.com

The unreserved and uncensored place to expose scams. Ripoff Report claims that their site (and your complaints) often help lawyers bolster their cases against unprofessional business practices, potentially changing the way they do business or getting compensation for wronged customers. This means that your complaining could be another consumer's salvation.

- Executive Bomb
  http://www.executivebomb.com

Unfortunately, sending a complaint to a generic customer service email address frequently results in nothing, or in a personal resolution with no tangible change in how the company conducts its business. Sometimes you have to go straight to the top to get results, and executivebomb .com will help you get there.

Search a company name to find the email convention for that company. Then look up the names of its customer experience executive or even the CEO and tell it like you see it. Oftentimes, they may not be aware of the inconvenience or injustice you've experienced. And hopefully, they take your words to heart and make some top-down changes.

- FTC Complaint Assistant
  http://www.ftccomplaintassistant.gov

Submit a complaint straight to the government. Complaints submitted to the FTC help the government prosecute companies for illegal business practices and involves law enforcement authorities worldwide.

- Pissed Consumer
  http://www.pissedconsumer.com

PissedConsumer.com is a great resource for consumer tips. But as the name suggests, it's the place to come as a pissed consumer. You can vent and express dissatisfaction. Then, PissedConsumer.com factors your complaint(s) into their Customer Satisfaction Index and shows which companies are the most hated.

- Complaints Board
  http://www.complaintsboard.com

Annoyed? Infuriated? Complaintsboard.com is the place to get it all out. Though it's not just venting at companies,

Complaintsboard.com is the aptly named forum for complaining. To combat the many tales of woe they receive,
the website also shares articles about companies and tips
for consumers and businesses.

- Measured Up
  http://www.measuredup.com

Want to talk to the big businesses that generally don't
seem to have time for little old you? Measured Up can be
your messenger, delivering your feedback to the company
(so that you don't have to call customer service).

- Consumerist Tipster app
  https://itunes.apple.com/us/app/consumerist-tipster/
  id443045014?mt=8

In conjunction with Consumerist.com, the tipster app lets
you use your smartphone to report any illegal or amoral
business practices that just won't fly (and the amazing
ones you'd like to share). Take a picture and forward it
to Consumerist.com; they'll post the "greatest hits" and
sometimes force the businesses to address their misstep.

OR USE SOCIAL MEDIA TO BE HEARD:

- Kelli B. Grant, "Want Customer Service? Complain on
  Twitter," *SmartMoney*, May 18, 2009
  http://www.smartmoney.com/spend/family-money/want
  -customer-service-post-your-complaint-on-twitter
- *Joe Manna*, "5 Ways to Complain Through Social
  Media"
  http://www.joemanna.com/blog/5-ways-to-complain
  -through-social-media

HERE ARE SOME OF THE TOP INTERNATIONAL COMPLAINT SITES:

- *Consumer Complaints* (Indian Consumer Complaints Forum)
  http://www.consumercomplaints.in
- The Consumerist
  http://www.consumerist.com
- *Core Centre* (Consumer Online Resource & Empowerment Centre)
  http://www.core.nic.in

IF NONE OF THAT WORKS, TAKE IT TO SMALL CLAIMS:

Small Claims Court is a place for you to try to take back what you believe you're owed. Filing a claim is more affordable and efficient than larger lawsuits, and you can probably represent yourself. Visit your state's government website for information on how to file a complaint and get your case heard.

5. Support Simple Start-Ups

Here are a couple we like the sounds of:
- Simple
  https://simple.com
- Minus
  https://minus.com

But there are many more small companies with great ideas that put the simple mentality at heart. They just need the customer base and capital to get a foothold.

For Businesses

We realize we may be sending some complaints your way. But as Bill Gates says, "Unhappy customers are your greatest source of learning." We suggest taking advantage of the unsolicited advice you're getting by way of social media and complaint forums. Here you not only have free and direct access to your customers, but you can take action to address their dissatisfaction and, perhaps, rescue the relationship. Often, handling a poor experience in a positive way can mean more to the customer than the original experience.

For Everybody

Get involved! These organizations and resources are ready and waiting.

- Consumer Financial Protection Bureau (CFPB)
  www.consumerfinance.gov

The Consumer Financial Protection Bureau is a wonderful new resource that puts the government on your side. Its mission is:

> to make markets for consumer financial products and service work for Americans whether they are applying for a mortgage, choosing among credit cards, or using any number of other consumer financial products. Above all, this means ensuring that consumers get the information they need to make the financial decisions they believe are best for themselves and their

families—that prices are clear up front, that risks are
visible, and that nothing is buried in fine print.

Sound good? We sure think so.

They're promising a three-pronged approach to tackle
consumer financial confusion and complexity from all
angles:

1. Educate: an informed consumer is the first line of
   defense against abusive practices.
2. Enforce: the CFPB supervises banks, credit unions, and
   other financial companies, and will enforce federal
   consumer financial laws.
3. Study: the CFPB gathers and analyzes available information to better understand consumers, financial services providers, and consumer financial markets.

Still think the government isn't listening? Take the CFPB's
complaint portal for a spin at www.consumerfinance
.gov and click on "Submit a Complaint." From July 2011
through September 2012, CFPB received 79,000 consumer
complaints regarding credit cards, banks, student loans,
and mortgages.

- The Center for Plain Language
  http://www.centerforplainlanguage.org

With the tag line "plain language is a civil right," the
Center for Plain Language is an advocacy group that
wants clear and understandable government and
business documents. This group is all about action—they
train English language abusers, award plain language
champions, and conduct and share research, give

workshops and presentations, and publish best practices for plain language.

- Common Good
  http://www.commongood.org

Common Good is a nonpartisan, nonprofit organization that thinks our legal system is failing and that "reclaiming responsibility requires a basic shift—where law sets boundaries for free choice instead of dictating choices for the lowest common denominator." Politicians need to stop passing the buck and using obsolete laws to dodge responsibility.

So out with the red tape, and in with the common good! After all, as the website's About Us section says, "People, not rules, make things happen." Go to their website to learn more about how Common Good is using common sense to promote their Start Over campaign.

- The Plain Language Action and Information Network (PLAIN)
  http://www.plainlanguage.gov

From the mouth of the beast: "Citizens deserve clear communications from their government." PLAIN is a group of federal employees across different government agencies who help the government fulfill that promise by encouraging clarity and transparency in government communications. With goals of saving federal agencies time and money and providing better service to Americans, PLAIN holds open meetings, offers editing services, sponsors seminars, critiques government documents, and gives writing training for federal employees.

Resources

- The Consumers Union (CU)
  www.consumersunion.org

The Consumers Union has been around the block. In the mid-1930s, when the ad world was booming, consumers "lacked a reliable source of information they could depend on to help them distinguish hype from fact and good products from bad ones." CU took on that role by doing the research, testing the products, and employing mystery shoppers.

You can become a more informed consumer by reading any of their incredibly popular publications.

- ConsumerReports.org
- *Consumer Reports,* the magazine
- *Consumer Reports on Health* (newsletter)
- ConsumerReportsHealth.org
- Consumer Reports Health Rating Center
- *Consumer Reports Money Adviser* (newsletter)

Join a community of over eight million readers, or even become part of their research base by completing their Annual Ballot & Questionnaire. We encourage you to at least visit ConsumerReports.org, a community of activists who use the Internet to instigate change while the Consumers Union lobbies, conducts outreach, and organizes grassroots campaigns.

- Consumers International (CI)
  http://www.consumersinternational.org

With a worldwide network of 220 member organizations, the nonprofit organization Consumers International is trying to start a movement to "put the rights of consumers at the heart of decision-making." By demanding reform in the laws that govern corporate behavior and condemning the behavior that harms, deceives, or abuses consumers, CI is a powerful watchdog and consumer advocate. They represent consumers when working with the United Nations (UN), World Health Organization (WHO), International Organization of Standardization (ISO), and the Food and Agriculture Organization (FAO), to make tangible international progress.

- The Financial Industry Regulatory Authority (FINRA)
  http://www.finra.org

FINRA's job is to protect investors and regulate, monitor, and discipline the securities industry. Like other organizations, they think of information as the strongest weapon. Go to their website or attend a public forum to learn more about saving, investing, and how FINRA is trying to create transparency in an industry known for its cloistering.

- Federal Trade Commission (FTC)
  http://ftc.gov

The FTC is a consumer watchdog that touches many facets of everyday American life. Its jurisdiction spans many sectors to ensure consumer protection and a fair market. This government commission is charged with law enforcement, advising legislatures and other agencies, and developing policy, research, and education for the consumer and the businessperson.

- PLAIN and PLAIN International
  http://www.plainlanguagenetwork.org

This Canadian-based organization called Plain Language Association International is on a mission to increase the use of plain language and the accessibility of communications in the most complex of industries—medicine, law, information management, education, and communications. It's a network of volunteers—professionals, organizations, and plain language advocates—who give their time to promote the use and development of plain language and network with their international members and other organizations.

- Clarity
  http://www.clarity-international.net

Finally, a set of lawyers who will speak to you in your language, not their legalese. Clarity International is a group of lawyers who advocate plain language writing and prove that it's possible to write in a way that is both legally precise and easy to understand. They publish a biannual journal and foster a community of like-minded lawyers and writers through their conferences, website, listserv, and networking.

- Consumer Federation of America (CFA)
  http://www.consumerfed.org

The Consumer Federation of America is an association of nonprofit consumer organizations that was established in 1968 to advance the consumer interest through research, advocacy, and education. Today, nearly three hundred of these groups participate in the federation and govern it through their representatives on the organization's Board of Directors.

Conducting conferences, publishing consumer education, advocating consumer-centric policy before government bodies, and researching consumer and corporate behavior, the CFA has become a powerhouse that collaborates with policymakers. Click on the "For Consumers" tab to read about their pro-consumer campaigns and explore their educational materials.

ACKNOWLEDGMENTS

We would like to thank the following individuals, companies, and organizations for their contributions in the form of interviews, work worthy of showcasing, and/or general support during the writing of this book. In some circumstances where we interviewed groups of individuals, we have cited only one or two individuals but greatly appreciate the time and effort of all who helped us find and applaud examples of simplification.

Deborah Adler, independent graphic designer (designer of
    Target prescription bottles and labels)
Robert Bartlett, lawyer
Gregg Bernstein, Savannah College of Art and Design
Diederiekje Bok and Hein Mevissen, John Doe,
    Amsterdam
Candy Chang, artist
Cleveland Clinic: Dr. James Merlino, Chief Experience
    Officer; Carmen Kestranek, Senior Director,
    Experience Intelligence; Sarah Sinclair, Executive
    Chief Nursing Officer; Donna Zabell, Senior Director,
    Employee Experience; Shelley Frost, Consumer Affairs

and Ombudsman Office; Mary Linda Rivera, Executive
Director, Office of Patient Experience; William
Peacock, Chief of Operations; Joe Patrnchak, Chief
Human Resources Officer
Neil Cohn, visual language teacher, Tufts University
ERGO Insurance: Hans Fabry, Director of Marketing;
Dr. David Stachon, CMO
David Geffen School of Medicine, UCLA
Philip K. Howard, Founder of Common Good
Professor Sheena Iyangar, author of *The Art of Choosing*
Arkadi Kuhlmann, CEO, ING Direct USA
Leanne Libert, former colleague at Siegel+Gale
Frank Luntz, author of *Words That Work*
John Maeda, President, Rhode Island School of
Design
Gino Menchini, Commissioner of the Department of
Information Technology and Telecommunications,
New York City
Daniel Oppenheimer, Professor of Psychology, Princeton
University
Andrea Ragnetti, formerly Chief Simplicity Officer,
Philips Electronics
Josh Reich, Founder, Simple
Daniel Schwarcz, Associate Professor of Law, University
of Minnesota
Professor Barry Schwarz, author of *The Paradox of
Choice*

Peter Sealey, author of *Simplicity Marketing: End Brand Complexity, Clutter, and Confusion*

Joseph Tainter, anthropologist, University of Utah

Jasper van Kujik, researcher, UT Delft, the Netherlands

Colin Ware, Director of Data Visualization Lab, University of New Hampshire

Ray Weaver, Professor, Harvard Business School

Susan Weinstock, Project Director, Safe Checking in the Electronic Age, Pew Charitable Trusts

Adrian Westaway, Vitamins Design and Invention Studio

We are particularly grateful to Warren Berger, who helped us draft the book. Since we were both so close to the subject, he interviewed us endlessly and pored over written material we had amassed over time to help find the kernels worth sharing. Distilling and clarifying volumes of material, he simplified a daunting task for us.

We owe another debt of gratitude to Christina Badalich Choi, a fresh-from-college Barnard graduate who worked with us as an editorial assistant during the summer of 2011. Her attention to detail, sharp eye, and calm demeanor brought organization and momentum to our writing process. We are happy to say that we snatched her up and brought her skills to our consulting practice. She is now an information architect in Siegel+Gale's Customer Experience practice.

We also want to acknowledge the inspiring work of the Customer Experience team of Siegel+Gale, in particular the groundbreakers who have helped define the practice of simplification: Maria Boos, Lori Cummings, Madge Dion, Matt DuBeau, Thomas Mueller, and Charlene Raytek.

ILLUSTRATION CREDITS

Figure 2.2. Global Brand Simplicity Index 2011. Prepared by Siegel+Gale, LLC.

Figure 3.1. Artwork created by Siegel+Gale, LLC.

Figure 4.1. Bloomberg Business app, Bloomberg Finance LP. From http://www.Bloomberg.com.

Figure 5.1. Prepared by Siegel+Gale, LLC for conference demonstration.

Figure 5.2. Prepared by Siegel+Gale, LLC for public discussion.

Figure 5.3. By Civic Center. Available at http://candychang .com/tenants-rights-flash-cards/.

Figure 5.4. By Vitamins, Design and Invention Studio. http:// www.vitaminsdesign.com.

Figure 5.5. Prototype prepared by Siegel+Gale, LLC as concept for student loan contract.

Figure 5.6a and 5.6b. Prototypes prepared by Siegel+Gale, LLC as concept.

Figure 5.7. From Jerome R. Joffman et al., "The Roulette Wheel: An Aid to Informed Decision Making," *PLoS Medicine*, June 2006.

Figure 5.8. Prototype prepared by Siegel+Gale, LLC based on
   public records.
Figure 6.1. By Smart Design.
Figure 6.2. From the MoMA exhibit "Talk to Me."
Figure 7.1. From http://www.bagcheck.com/terms.
Figure 7.2. By Pew Charitable Trusts.
Figure 7.3. Available at http://www.cfpb.gov.
Figure 7.4. From the U.S. Department of Education.

NOTES

Chapter 1: The Crisis of Complexity

1. "Beware of Bogus Phone Bill Fees," *Consumer Reports*, August 2012.
2. Dawn Fallik, "$5 Million Jury Award in Death of Year-Old Boy," *Philadelphia Inquirer*, July 25, 2006.
3. Susan H. Corey, Jeffrey Smith, and Daniel J. Sheehan, "Physician Signatures," *Southern Medical Journal*, August 2008.
4. Leander Kahney, "John Sculley on Steve Jobs: The Full Interview," *Cult of Mac*, October 14, 2010.
5. *People* magazine, May 22, 1978.
6. David Segal, "It's Complicated: Making Sense of Complexity," *New York Times*, May 2, 2010.
7. Paul Johnson, "In Business, Simplicity Is Golden," Forbes.com, March 16, 2009, www.forbes.com/forbes/2009/0316/017_current_events.html.
8. From our interview with Daniel Schwarcz, June 9, 2011.
9. Segal, "It's Complicated."
10. David Kocieniewski, "I.R.S. Ombudsman Calls for a Broad Overhaul of Tax Regulations," *New York Times*, January 5, 2011.
11. *Newsmakers*, C-SPAN, January 10, 2010.
12. Adam Liptak, "Justices Long on Words but Short on Guidance," *New York Times*, November 18, 2010.
13. David Leonhardt, "Buyer, Be Aware: What We Don't Understand as Consumers Could Really Hurt Us," *New York Times Magazine*, August 15, 2010.
14. Kenneth Chang, "A Challenge to Make Science Crystal Clear," *New York Times*, March 5, 2012.

Chapter 2: Breakthrough Simplicity

1. The story of online banking start-up Simple is based on our interviews with founder Josh Reich, August 2011.
2. Kristian Andersen, "Designing a New Bank Experience," *KA+A*, June 24, 2011.
3. Heather Landy, "Customer to Banks: Simple Sells," *American Banker*, March 16, 2011.
4. Gregory M. Lamb, "A Fast Rate of Return," *Christian Science Monitor*, May 15, 2006.
5. Bruce Horovitz, "Marketers Such as Starbucks Discover That Simple Sells," *USA Today*, October 2, 2009.
6. Joe Brancatelli, "Southwest Airlines' Seven Secrets for Success," Portfolio .com, July 8, 2008.
7. From a study in *Yankelovich Monitor Minute*, February 2005.
8. Kevin Ransom, "Reign of the Plain: Survey Finds Gen Ys Prefer Brand Simple," MediaPost.com, April 20, 2007.
9. Survey conducted in July 2010, published at HarrisInteractive.com, September 24, 2010.
10. More on this can be found in Lew McCreary, "Kaiser Permanente's Innovation on the Front Lines," *Harvard Business Review*, September 2010.
11. From Siegel+Gale survey of 1,214 Americans conducted between December 29, 2008, and January 5, 2009, and released on January 14, 2009.
12. Joe Davidson, "Time for a Plain-Language Revolution," *Washington Post*, October 30, 2009.
13. The survey is explained in Aliya Sternstein, "Americans Give Low Marks to Obama Transparency Effort at Agencies," NextGov.com, October 20, 2010.

Chapter 3: Empathize

1. Our section on Cleveland Clinic is based on on-site visits to the clinic and interviews conducted there with, among others, Dr. James Merlino, the chief experience officer, November 9, 2011.
2. Steve Szilagyi, "The Patient Experience," *Cleveland Clinic Magazine*, Winter 2011.

3. "Customer Rage: It's Not Always About the Money," *Knowledge@W.P. Carey* (blog), November 23, 2005, quoting the annual "customer rage" study by Customer Care Alliance.
4. From, among other reports, Lora Kolodny, "Study: 82% of U.S. Consumers Bail on Brands after Bad Customer Service," *TechCrunch*, October 13, 2010.
5. From our interviews with Oppenheimer, August 19, 2011.
6. E. B. Boyd, "For Brands, Being Human Is the New Black," FastCompany .com, August 29, 2011.
7. Based on our interviews with ING Direct CEO Arkadi Kuhlmann.
8. Ann Carrns, "Capital One's Response to Outrage over ING Direct Purchase," *New York Times*, June 22, 2011.
9. The story of IDEO's hospital ceiling redesign is recounted in Paul Bennett, "Listening Lessons: Make Consumers Part of the Design Process by Tuning In," *Advertising Age Point*, March 2006.
10. Gregory R. Istre et al., "Increasing the Use of Child Restraints in Motor Vehicles in a Hispanic Neighborhood," *American Journal of Public Health*, July 2002.
11. From B. L. Ochman, "Don't Call Us! 47 of the Fortune 50 Have No Phone Number on Their Home Page," *What's Next?* (blog), June 25, 2011.
12. Jamie Lywood, Merlin Stone, and Yuksel Ekinci, "Customer Experience and Profitability: An Application of the Empathy Rating Index (ERIC) in UK Call Centres," *Journal of Database Marketing and Customer Strategy Management* 16, no. 3 (2009): 207–14.

Chapter 4: Distill

1. The Google profile is based on our interviews with Marissa Mayer, the company's former director of consumer web products (who has since moved to Yahoo!). This section also refers to our 2011 Global Brand Simplicity Index, which ranked Google number one in delivering a simple experience.
2. Excerpted from "'Focusing is about saying no'—Steve Jobs (WWDC'97)," YouTube video, 3:06, from Steve Jobs's closing keynote at Apple's World

Wide Developer Conference in 1997, posted by Davide "Folletto" Casali on June 26, 2011, http://youtube/H8eP99neOVs.

3. Maeda's quote appeared in Nicole La Porte, "In the School of Innovation, Less Is Often More," *New York Times*, November 6, 2011.

4. James Sherwood, "Most 'Malfunctioning' Gadgets Work Just Fine, Report Claims," June 3, 2008, www.reghardware.com.

5. Taken from our interviews with van Kuijk.

6. The Flip Video story draws on a number of sources, including Warren Berger's interviews with Smart Design's Richard Whitehall for this book; the guest post written by Smart Design's Nasahn Sheppard in *Pogue's Posts*, David Pogue's technology blog in the *New York Times*, July 7, 2011; Pogue's *New York Times* column titled "Camcorder Brings Zen to the Shoot," March 20, 2008; and Patrick Mannion, "Under the Hood: Flip Ultra Camcorder an Ode to Clean Design," *EE Times*, February 18, 2008.

7. Gareth Kay, "Reducing Friction," April, 18, 2011, http://garethkay.typepad.com, citing a quote from Jack Dorsey in an article from MIT's *Technology Review*.

8. From our interviews with Hein Mevissen and Diederiekje Bok.

9. From our interviews with Arlene Harris.

10. From our interview with Peter Sealey of the Sausalito Group marketing consultancy.

11. Beth Kowitt, "Inside Trader Joe's," *Fortune*, September 6, 2010.

12. Martin Lindstrom, "A Store with Only 3 Products and Other Cases for Simplicity," FastCompany.com, August 29, 2011.

13. Carmen Nobel, "A New Model for Business: The Museum," Harvard Business School's *Working Knowledge* newsletter, August 15, 2011.

14. David Pogue, "More Grumbling at Facebook," *New York Times*, October 20, 2011.

15. Chris Taylor, "Facebook Is Getting Too Damn Complicated," *Mashable*, September 30, 2011.

16. Pogue, "More Grumbling at Facebook."

17. The Pandora analysis draws from a number of sources, including Rob Walker, "The Song Decoders," *New York Times Magazine*, October 18, 2009, as well as an interview with Westergren that appeared on the website of Greylock Partners titled "The Entrepreneur Questionnaire: Tim Westergren," July 28, 2011, greylockvc.com.

Chapter 5: Clarify

1. Deborah Adler's story is drawn primarily from Warren Berger's interviews with her for this book.
2. Michelle Andrews, "New Ideas to Help People Take Medications Correctly," *Los Angeles Times*, March 21, 2011.
3. Deborah Franklin, "And Now, a Warning About Labels," *New York Times*, October 25, 2005.
4. Gina Kolata, "Side Effects? These Drugs Have a Few," *New York Times*, June 5, 2011.
5. Irene Etzkorn, "When Life Depends on Clear Instructions," Siegel+Gale, citing study conducted by Uniformed Services University of the Health Sciences in Maryland, 2003.
6. William Langewiesche, "The Devil at 37,000 Feet," *Vanity Fair*, January 2009.
7. From Warren Berger's interview with Tufts University's Neil Cohn.
8. Cheyenne Hopkins, "Banks' Litigation Fears Clash with CFPB Goal of Simpler Card Disclosures," *American Banker*, October 7, 2010.
9. Steven Leckart, "Blood Simple," *Wired*, December 2010.
10. From our interview with Adrian Westaway, September 8, 2011.
11. From our interview with Dr. David Stachon, July 2011, CMO, ERGO.
12. From our interview with Rob Wallace, June 6, 2006.
13. From Warren Berger's interview with Lee Clow.
14. From our interview with Amanda Bach, June 6, 2006.
15. From Warren Berger's interview with Colin Ware.
16. Natasha Singer, "When the Data Struts Its Stuff," *New York Times*, April 2, 2011.
17. Bob Greenberg, "Seeing Is Believing," *Adweek*, October 25, 2010.
18. Jerome R. Joffman et al., "The Roulette Wheel: An Aid to Informed Decision Making," *PLoS Medicine*, June 2006.
19. The story behind this was reported in Elisabeth Bumiller, "We Have Met the Enemy and He Is PowerPoint," *New York Times*, April 26, 2010.
20. Elizabeth Warren, interview with David Brancaccio, *NOW*, PBS, week of January 2, 2009.
21. An excellent recounting of the history of this term can be found in David Keene, "Gobbledygook's Persistence," *The Hill*, February 23, 2009.
22. Arthur Levitt, "A Word to Wall Street: 'Plain English,' Please," *Wall Street Journal*, April 2, 2011.

23. From "A Clarion Call for Transparency," survey by Siegel+Gale, February 2009.
24. Diana Middleton, "Students Struggle for Words," *Wall Street Journal*, March 3, 2011.
25. Claude Singer, "More Horror from Lionsgate Entertainment Corp.," *Brandsinger*, September 3, 2011.
26. Buffett wrote this in the introduction to the 1998 *SEC Plain English Handbook*. It is cited in Joanne Locke, "A History of Plain Language in the United States Government," www.PlainLanguage.gov.
27. Gadi Dechter, "ANALYSIS: Information Overload," *Government Executive*, October 2011.
28. Lucy Kellaway, "Words to Describe the Glory of Apple," FinancialTimes .com, September 19, 2010.
29. Daniel M. Oppenheimer, "Consequences of Erudite Vernacular Utilized Irrespective of Necessity: Problems with Using Long Words Needlessly," *Applied Cognitive Psychology* 20 (2006).

Chapter 6: Top-Down and Bottom-Up

1. This is based on our visit to "The Simplicity Event," hosted by Philips in New York in 2006, as well as our interviews with the company's CMO, Andrea Ragnetti.
2. "Capitalizing on Complexity," IBM study, 2010.
3. Sian Harrington, "$1.2 Billion Each: The Hidden Cost of People Complexity to the Top 200," *HR*, September 6, 2011.
4. From an interview with Jobs in *BusinessWeek*, October 12, 1994.
5. Jessica E. Vascellaro, "Tim Cook on Hardware, Apple's Structure and Being 'Simpletons,'" *Digits* (blog), *Wall Street Journal*, February 16, 2012.
6. Adam Bryant, "Early Access as a Fast Track to Learning" (includes interview of David Barger, president of JetBlue), *New York Times*, September 25, 2011.
7. Lee discussed the creation of the OXO measuring cup in his speech at the GEL Conference in New York, April 2008; the speech can be seen at http:// vimeo.com/3200945.
8. From "68 Rules? No, Just 3 Are Enough," *Corner Office* interview by Adam Bryant, *New York Times*, November 21, 2009.

9. Lucy Kellaway, "Business English: I've Found the Worst Employee Handbook Ever," *Financial Times*, August 27, 2007.
10. "The CEO, Now Appearing on YouTube," *Corner Office* interview by Adam Bryant, *New York Times*, May 9, 2009.
11. Christa Avampato, "An Interview with Alex Lee, CEO of OXO," *New York Business Strategies Examiner*, March 15, 2009.
12. Steven Johnson, "Invisible City," *Wired*, November 2010.
13. Lisa Fickenscher, "Now, Opening a Restaurant Is as Easy as NBAT," *Crains New York*, January 3, 2012.
14. Steven Johnson, "What a Hundred Million Calls to 311 Reveal About New York," *Wired*, November 10, 2010, http://www.wired.com/magazine/2010/11/ff_311_new_york/all/.

Chapter 7: Where Do We Go from Here?

1. From *ABC News* report on protests of bank fees, reported by Susanna Kim and Matt Gutman, November 1, 2011.
2. Stuart Pfeifer and E. Scott Reckard, "One Facebook Post Becomes National Movement to Abandon Big Banks," *Los Angeles Times*, November 4, 2011.
3. From *NBC News* report on student loans, broadcast May 17, 2011.
4. From Siegel+Gale's Financial Award Letter Survey, conducted June 2008.

INDEX

·················

Index

Pandora Media, Inc. (Internet radio),
    98–99
path of least resistance, 13–14
persuasion, theory of, 143–46
Pew Charitable Trusts, 183–86
Philips Electronics, 83, 149–53, 168–69
Pissed Consumer (website), 195
plain language movement. *See also*
    clarity/clarify; communications
  benefits to business, 134–35
  cognitive fluency and, 135–37
  corporate culture resistance, 142–43
  habit of company-speak, 137–42
  health/healthcare, 56–57
  about the origins, xii, 130–31
  overcoming jargon, 21–22
  politicization of, 131–34
  simplification models, 182–86
  U.S. government and, 42–43
Plain Writing Act of 2010, 43, 132
PLoS Medicine (journal), 127
Pogue, David, 96
Powell, Colin, 150
Practicing Law Institute, xii
privacy/privacy policy, 65, 71
product design
  keep it simple, 84–88
  overcoming the silo effect, 164–65
  ripple effect, 169–70
  simplification and, 151–52
product packaging, 123–24
Pure Digital Technologies, Inc., 84–88

Quicken (software), 169–70

Radin, Margaret Jane, 199
Ragnatti, Andrea, 151–53
Reagan, Ronald, 131–32
red tape, 8–9
Reggio, Theo, 163–64
Reich, Josh, 24–28
religious and cultural beliefs, 71–72
resources and websites, 201–15
Reynolds, Johua, 81

"rhetorical theory," 143–46
Roosevelt, Eleanor, 179
Rosling, Hans, 125–26

Safeway Supermarkets, 92
Samsung Electronics, 89–91
Sausalito Group (consultants), 92
Schiro, James J., 163
Schumacher, E. F., 25
Schwarcz, Daniel, 16
Sculley, John, 7
Sealey, Peter, 92–93
Segal, David, 14
Segall, Ken, 199
Shelley, Percy Bysshe, 54
Sheppard, Nasahn, 85, 88
Shulman, Douglas, 17
Siegel, Alan (aka "Mr. Plain language), 9
Simple Bank, 24–28
simplicity. *See also* breakthrough
    simplicity; clutter; complexity
  defined, 6–8
  demographics, 38–40
  Google search engine, 78–81
  lessons learned, 10–13
  as "luxury" alternative, 34–37
  paying a premium for, 29–30
  steps for taking control, 201
Simplicity Lab, 10
simplicity premium, 29–30
simplification. *See also* clarity/clarify;
    distill/distillation; empathy/
    empathize
  as academic discipline, xii–xiv, 9–10
  applies to all communications, 10–11
  automation and technology, 76–77
  avoiding faux simplicity, 192–95
  books and resources for, 199–215
  data is not information, 109–10
  disclosure models, 183–86
  identifying the essence of, 48–49
  minimalist product design, 84–88
  as a philosophy (way of life), 7–8
  when less is more, 30–31, 82–84, 91–94

235

Index

Index